ONE TO ONE:
A PRACTICAL GUIDE
TO FRIENDSHIP
EVANGELISM

One to One

A PRACTICAL GUIDE TO FRIENDSHIP EVANGELISM

Terry Wardle

Christian Publications

CAMP HILL, PENNSYLVANIA

Christian Publications
3825 Hartzdale Drive, Camp Hill, PA 17011

The mark of 🕇 *vibrant faith*

ISBN: 0-87509-423-6
LOC Catalog Card Number: 89–62285
© 1989 by Christian Publications
All rights reserved
Printed in the United States of America

94 93 92   5 4 3 2

Cover photo
© COMSTOCK, Inc./Michael Stuckey

To my father and mother,
Howard and Norma Wardle.
I have rested in your love
every day of my life.

CONTENTS

PREFACE

WE WERE SITTING AT THE DINNER TABLE savoring a wonderful meal. The presence of an old college friend made this a special evening. I had not seen Steve for several years, and we enjoyed the opportunity to get reacquainted. Cheryl and the children listened and laughed as we remembered days gone by. During a quiet moment Steve looked at me and said, "Terry, you're different. You're not the person I knew back in college. What's happened?"

My friend's observation was right on. I *was* different. My attitudes, appetites and actions had gone through a radical transformation. Anyone who knew me could attest to that. As I looked at Steve, preparing to respond to his question, two words kept flashing in my mind—friendship and the gospel, two powerful forces that can radically change a person. Each one had been at work in my life, and as a result I was a different person!

I doubt whether I could adequately describe the impact friendship has had on my life. In part, whatever I am today is a result of some special people. Their love, acceptance, encouragement and support has literally changed me. People like Brad and Evan who gave love when I was absolutely unlovable. Or John and Donn, men of God who stood at my side during the early stages of faith and ministry. And, of course, Gene, who to this day models the Christian life in an incredible way. David, Andy, Mark—the list goes on and on. Their impact on my life will last as long as I draw breath. Friendship is that powerful.

But the gospel of Jesus Christ is even more powerful. When a person opens his or her life to its work, things are never again the same. I still remember the night Jesus entered my life. It was in a small apartment at Geneva College. Several friends knelt in support as I surrendered my heart to Christ. At the time I did not fully realize what was about to happen. But every day since, the gospel has been at work within, transforming my life. The Lord has faithfully loved me, yet at the same time challenged me to change. His Spirit has been at work cleansing, remaking, instructing and infilling. Old things keep fading away; the Lord is doing something new. People who have given their lives to Christ know what I am talking about. The gospel is an invitation to radical transformation.

This book will challenge you to bring together these two forces in a ministry of friendship evangelism. Build life-changing relationships with non-Christians and at the same time share the transforming message of Jesus Christ. People today are lonely, hurting deep within, convinced no one truly cares about them. Thousands upon thousands are lost now and forever because they do not know the Savior, Jesus Christ. But as the Lord's disciple you can make a dramatic difference in their lives. Become a friendship evangelist. This book, by God's grace, will show you why and how.

The first chapter addresses the question, "What is evangelism anyway?" When properly understood, outreach through friendship is a valid, nonoffensive ministry. In chapters 2 and 3 we will consider the message and motives behind all evangelism. Chapter 4 focuses upon the believer's devotion to God—an indispensable ingredient in effective Christian service. Chapter 5 looks at the Holy Spirit's part in the process. Friendship is the theme of chapters 6 and 7. We will discuss the advantages of friendship evangelism and share practical suggestions for building relationships with non-Christians. Chapter 8 gives instruction on how to share the gospel, and in 9 we will discuss the importance of follow-up. In the conclusion, I have set forth a strategy for a friendship evangelism ministry in the local church. This book was written because friendship evangelism changed my life. But more important, it was written because I believe it can, through you, change the world!

I would like to express my deep appreciation to H. Robert Cowles, retired executive vice president of Christian Publications. He is a true friend and throughout this project has offered encouragement and support. Bob has left his mark on my life and on the pages of this book.

I also want to thank Lois Volstad, who enthusiastically typed, read and retyped the original manuscript. She is a special "second mile" friend. In addition, I am grateful to my administrative assistant, Shirley Hahn, and David Hall who reviewed the follow-up material in chapter 9.

Most important, I am indebted to Cheryl, Aaron, Cara and Emily. Their love, encouragement and patience helped me through some long nights of writing. More than my wife and children, they are my dearest "friends."

All the stories in this book are true. But I chose in some cases to use fictitious names as a way of protecting some special people.

Friendship Evangelism and You

MY SON AARON IS A SOCCER FANATIC! He spends every spare moment playing, watching or reading about the sport. Even as I write he is at a soccer camp, investing hours sharpening his skills for the upcoming season. Ask Aaron what he likes best about soccer, and he will undoubtedly say, "the games." He loves the thrill and challenge of competition. But he does *not* like the long hours spent in reviewing fundamentals. Aaron consistently complains that practices are boring. His wise coach, however, knows that success or failure depends on mastering the basics. For weeks before the season begins, Coach Gray works on elementary skills and plays until they become second nature to his team. He knows game time will come soon enough.

This principle holds true for every important discipline, including evangelism. A good, healthy evangelistic ministry is built upon a proper understanding of basics. While not as exciting as actually sharing the gospel, fundamentals are essential to long-term effectiveness. Therefore, we will begin with basics. And the most foundational issue of all is the definition of the word *evangelism*.

Definition

"Just what is evangelism anyway?" Each year I begin my evangelism class with that basic question. Interestingly, even among seminary students, the most common answers reflect an incomplete understanding at this rudimentary level. Responses often include the following:

> Evangelism is . . .
> passing out tracts
> holding a crusade
> warning people of eternal judgment
> sharing the Four Spiritual Laws
> confronting people with the gospel
> being a good person
> asking people, "Are you saved?"
> altar calls at the close of a service

While each response may reflect certain aspects of evangelism, the answers are incomplete. George Hunter, professor and dean of the E. Stanley Jones School of Evangelism and World Mission, perceptively commented, "Most people swear by the word evangelism or swear at it."[1] Similarly, author George Sweazey states,

> Words are fragile things, easily damaged. The word evangelism has been spoiled for many church people. They associate it with the shouter who makes a career of cheapening religion, or with the zealot who demands, "Brother, are you a Christian?" They may have the uneasy feeling that it is something they ought to be doing, but their very flesh recoils from the thought."[2]

Several evangelical authors have provided helpful

definitions of evangelism. While varying to some degree, they will help shape our basic understanding of outreach.

> Evangelism in the strict sense is proclaiming the Good News of salvation to men and women with a view to their conversion to Christ and incorporation in His Church.[3]

> Evangelism is communicating the gospel of Jesus Christ with the immediate intent of converting unbelievers to faith in Christ, and with the ultimate intent of instructing the convert in the Word of God so that he can become a mature believer.[4]

> The process whereby a person tells other people the gospel of the Lord Jesus Christ in an attempt to persuade them to put their faith in Jesus as their Lord and Savior.[5]

> To evangelize is to communicate the gospel in such a way that men and women have a valid opportunity to accept Jesus Christ as Lord and Savior and become responsible members of His Church.[6]

You will note that each definition highlights three important aspects of biblical evangelism. First, we learn what people should be doing in evangelism—they are to communicate the gospel of Jesus Christ. *Evangelism is proclaiming, in clear, understandable terms, the message of salvation in Jesus Christ.* True evangelism occurs only when that good news is being shared. Regardless of format—whether sermon, testimony, gospel outline or song—evangelism involves communication.

Second, we see why this communication is so important. *Every person should have a valid opportunity to receive Christ as Lord and Savior.* How clear Paul's words are in Romans 10:13-14: "Everyone who calls on the name of the Lord will be saved. How, then, can they call on the one they have not believed in? And how can they believe in the one of whom they have not heard? And how can they hear without someone preaching to them?" The implication is obvious. Evangelism involves proclaiming the gospel, giving people of every tribe and nation a valid opportunity to say yes to God's eternal gift.

Third, *the goal of evangelism is Christian discipleship.* Jesus told His followers to "make disciples" (Matthew 28:18-20). This is the Great Commission of Christ to His church, the end toward which all evangelistic efforts are directed. It is not enough that the message of salvation is communicated. God wants unbelievers to become faithful followers of Christ. And this requires both spiritual growth and incorporation into Christ's church as responsible members. The goal of evangelism is not a decision but rather, a true disciple.

What is evangelism? At its most basic level it is *communicating the Good News of salvation to men and women everywhere, giving them a valid opportunity to receive Jesus Christ as Lord and Savior and to become faithful, responsible members of His church.*

This will be our working definition of evangelism. Let us now discuss the necessary characteristics of evangelistic ministries faithful to this foundational understanding. I will address these characteristics under the headings Presence, Proclamation, Persuasion, Power.

C. Peter Wagner, professor of church growth at Fuller Theological Seminary, states that healthy evangelism is characterized by three important elements: presence, proclamation and persuasion.[7] Wagner illustrates these three "Ps" by likening them to three stories of a house.

3-P
PERSUASION
People are discipled

2-P
PROCLAMATION
People hear the gospel and understand

1-P
PRESENCE
People are loved and helped

The foundation of evangelism is presence. Simply stated, presence involves establishing helping and loving relationships with the unsaved. Proclamation, the second story, represents actually communicating the good news of salvation to others. Persuasion identifies the final goal of evangelism—discipleship. At this level individuals decide to act, responding to God's message of salvation. Wagner emphasizes, and rightly so, that all three elements are necessary if evangelism is to be effective.

I would like to add a fourth "P" to Wagner's formula—power. Only the Holy Spirit generates the power that makes evangelism effective. If they are to be effective, evangelistic efforts must be Spirit-led and empowered. He alone makes the gospel light shine forth. As such, Christians must consider the relationship of the Holy Spirit to evangelism.

Presence

George had disengaged from society. For 17 years he did not work, seldom stepped out of the house and virtually never left his yard. He was a recluse, an eccentric and an embarrassment to his family. George's wife and son were faithful church members, well liked and respected in the community. Yet, they had been scarred by George's behavior. Despite efforts to get help, things were steadily deteriorating.

George had often been the object of well-intentioned evangelistic efforts. From time to time pastors and church members would visit, hoping to share the gospel of salvation with him. Invariably their contact with George was unpleasant. He was not interested in church and told them not to return. George had built an impenetrable wall around his ever-dwindling world.

In the late 1970s I was appointed pastor of the church where George's family attended. Even before

I arrived, the former pastor told me about George. Experience had left him pessimistic, and he felt the situation was hopeless. Sadly, his attitude affected me. It was some time before I thought of visiting George. After all, I was not anxious for rejection or confrontation.

In the course of visiting all of the church families, I made an appointment to call on George's wife and son. I had no intention, however, of saying a word to George. When the evening arrived, George's son John met me at the door, visibly excited that I had come. He took me to the living room where his mother was seated. George, I thought, was not there.

The three of us talked for some time. I shared my background and at one point mentioned that I enjoyed hunting. Suddenly, a voice from the other room said, "I used to hunt." It was George! He had been sitting there listening to the conversation. My confession seemed to strike a chord, opening George to a small, yet positive response. I was both startled and encouraged.

For several days afterward, my mind was on George and his words, "I used to hunt." I decided to gather a number of sportsman magazines and take them to his home. Later, I stopped with snapshots of a hunting trip and a venison roast. It was not long before I was making regular visits, sharing great conversations with my new-found friend. Our times together were always friendly and pleasant.

Only after several months did I begin to cautiously, yet clearly, share the message of Jesus Christ. While not making an immediate response, George always listened. Words could never describe the joy I felt one Sunday when I looked out into the congregation and saw George. Before long his whole world began to change. George had opened up to the transforming message of Jesus Christ.

I share this story, which could be illustrated by countless other examples, to emphasize an evangelistic principle. Effective outreach begins when Christians penetrate the world around them. They must establish loving relationships with the unchurched. Shouting the gospel from a safe distance does not work. True evangelism involves identifying, touching and helping the lost people of this world. Christian presence means earning the right to share the gospel by showing that you care. Presence opens the door for proclaiming God's good news.

The local church faces a problem. Too often people find Christ and then retreat from the non-Christian world. At times they are advised to sever relationships with previous friends. Many Christians believe that such relationships entice people back into a life of sin. Certainly "backsliding" is a problem, but the answer is not radical separation. Rather, as author Rebecca Pippert points out, Christians must maintain a "radically different" lifestyle while "radically identifying" with the world.[8]

John Stott, British pastor and church leader, calls Christians to be "holy worldly." Again, the emphasis is on the balance between a biblical lifestyle and involvement in the secular world.

The greatest example of this evangelistic approach was our Lord Jesus. He radically identified with people while maintaining His radical difference. Instead of writing God's plan of redemption across the skies, Christ became one of us. He built friendships, cared for the hurting and touched the broken of the world. At the same time, He was perfectly holy. He walked in oneness with God—a true light in the darkness. He told us to follow His example when He said, "As the Father has sent me, I am sending you" (John 20:21b).

Evangelism begins not by disengaging from society but by establishing a beachhead of love among the unchurched. Christians must penetrate the world around them, relating, caring, helping, listening and touching. We must build meaningful friendships with our unchurched neighbors. By focusing on common interests, we can establish bridges of trust. In time the message of salvation will cross from one heart to the other. This is the foundation of effective evangelism: establishing a Christian presence with non-Christian friends and neighbors.

Proclamation

There are two Greek words used in the New Testament that influence our understanding of evangelism. The first is *euangelion*. This means *good message*. In the New Testament it refers to the message of salvation in Christ—the story that details the glorious account of Jesus, who died for our sin and rose in victory, bringing eternal life to all who believe.

The second word is a verb form of the same word, *euangelizomai*. As you can guess, it means *to announce good news*. This verb occurs frequently in the New Testament. It instructs Christians to announce this "good message of Jesus Christ" everywhere.

Evangelism is more than believing the gospel, though. It is also more than living the gospel. Biblical evangelism involves telling the gospel to others, announcing the good news of salvation. Proclamation is the critical second story of our 4-P evangelism illustration. Paraphrasing Paul in Romans 10:14, "How will people hear the good news if we don't tell them?"

Martha Corbin was attending the first friendship evangelism class held in her church. She was a godly woman with a sincere faith in Jesus Christ. When people were in need, Martha was always there—a true Christian example. During that first class, students were asked to share their thoughts about witnessing. Common fears and apprehensions quickly came to the surface. In the midst of this discussion Martha commented, "I believe we witness by our lives, *not* our words."

At first hearing, this statement sounds powerfully true. After all, Jesus called us to "let your light shine before men, that they may see your good deeds and praise your Father in heaven" (Matthew 5:16). The criticism that Christians are hypocrites comes because many claim to follow Christ, but live like pagans. Yet, in truth, Martha's insight was incomplete and imbalanced. Evangelism demands a witness of our lives *and* our words. Like two wings of a plane, both are absolutely necessary if evangelism is to get off the ground.

Certainly a caring, Christian lifestyle is important. This, by itself though, simply tells people you are different. A lifestyle does not help a person understand *why* you are different. Nor can a nonbeliever perceive God's plan of salvation and the steps to faith by observing the way you live. Communicating the gospel means telling others the good news in clear, understandable terms. This demands that the witness become familiar with the gospel, familiar enough to freely share it with others. Evangelism involves the second P—proclamation.

Several years ago I was involved in a discussion with an officer of a leading denomination. He was speaking about the thousands of dollars being spent by his group on evangelism. I asked him to describe their evangelism strategy. He listed projects such as feeding the hungry, health care programs, literacy campaigns and agricultural improvement efforts. Certainly all this is good and vital to our mission as God's people. But I had to ask, "How many people heard the gospel of Christ and came to a saving faith?" His answer was startling: "We do not believe that to be a necessary ingredient of evangelism."

Let us be clear at this point. Touching people where they hurt is critical. It is a necessary facet of a healthy evangelism strategy. Even more, it is part of being a caring human being. But presence ministries alone do not equal evangelism. Presence without proclamation is nothing more than humanization. And in evangelism, humanization is not enough! Evangelism means *to announce good news*. Any evangelism without announcement is incomplete and eternally inadequate.

But before we get too critical at this point, remember that evangelical Christians often have the opposite problem. Ignoring the hurts and needs of others, we shout the gospel from a safe and respectable distance. We offer tracts to starving people, hoping they will "prepare for eternity," though they are dying today. True evangelism involves both! Christians *must* reach out and actually care about the needs of others. Upon this foundation, we *must* announce the life-giving message of salvation in Jesus Christ! Evangelism is presence *and* proclamation!

Persuasion

Before Jesus ascended into heaven, He gave His followers clear instructions to make disciples of all nations. This is the imperative within the Great Commission (Matthew 28:18-20). As we discussed earlier, making a disciple is the goal of all evangelistic efforts. In our 4-P model this element is called persuasion. The measuring rod of biblical evangelism is not "how many people have heard." Rather it is "how many disciples have been made." Just as the goal of fishing is catching fish, the goal of evangelism is making disciples!

Persuasion really implies perseverance. It is not enough to simply help a person (1-P), or to tell them the gospel message (2-P). 3-P evangelism keeps persevering until a decision is made. Certainly this implies sensitivity, gentleness and a respect for any person who openly rejects Christ's offer. But the goal of true evangelism is still the same—discipleship. Jesus did not die so that we could simply "announce good news." He gave his life to actually set people free from the bondage of sin and death. Jesus Christ wants disciples.

There are hard-hitting implications of this evangelistic stance. Effectiveness will not be measured by the number of people who have heard the message. Rather, evaluation will be based on the effectiveness of a program in winning people to Christ. For many churches and evangelistic organizations, this will demand serious reexamination of their methods. Let me illustrate.

John Carter Adams is manager of the New York Bible Society. For several years he has, through NYBS, provided Scripture portions for evangelistic efforts in the city of New York. In 1987 the NYBS participated in a massive saturation evangelism program. The effort involved 10 parachurch organizations and 35 local congregations. Two thousand eight hundred evangelists, mostly college and high school students from across the United States, came to New York City and distributed 1 million Scripture portions. These were provided by NYBS at a cost of $23,000. In addition, tens of thousands of dollars were spent on transportation and housing for these "evangelists."

According to an extensive study by Adams and his associate, Scott Rigby, 6,000 people registered decisions for Christ. This was 6,000 in response to the 1 million Scripture portions shared. But Adams and Rigby were not just interested in decisions. They wanted to know how many disciples were made. Further research revealed that less than 200 of the 6,000 were presently involved in local churches as a result of these efforts. Certainly those 200 are precious and priceless to Christ, but the bottom line of all this energy, effort and financial support is less than impressive. I asked John his reaction to these findings. His response? Fright!

Some would argue that many good things came out of this effort, and that is true. Hundreds of young people were trained to share their faith; churches became more sensitized to evangelism; and one million people were exposed to the gospel.

But remember, in a 4-P evangelistic strategy, the goal is not training, spiritual vitality or announcement. The goal is discipleship—nothing more and nothing less.

Interestingly, Adams and Rigby's conclusion supports the basic thesis of this book. Friendship evangelism is the most effective way to reach, win and incorporate people into the church of Jesus Christ. They conclude:

> Churches who report the highest amounts of church growth also are more likely to report that their membership is actively involved in pursuing friendship relationships with non-Christians in the area. It is through these close relationships that people are brought to Christ. *If a contact is going to grow into a disciple of Christ, it will be largely the result of a local Christian body that is willing to form a lasting, loving relationship with that contact.*[9]

Power

Effective evangelism does not take place apart from the person and work of the Holy Spirit. He must be actively involved at every point in leading people to Jesus Christ. Understanding the role of the Holy Spirit is necessary if Christians want to be effective in evangelism.

Look at the life of Christ. From conception to ascension, the Holy Spirit was involved in His life. In Luke 1 and 2 the writer states that the Holy Spirit moved in the incarnation. In Luke 3 and 4 we read that the Holy Spirit anointed Christ at the start of His ministry. He then guided Jesus into the wilderness where He faced Satan's temptation. Luke 4:14 tells us that Jesus returned from the wilderness, "in the power of the Holy Spirit," to begin a public ministry of preaching, healing and deliverance. It was by the power of God's Spirit that Jesus worked signs, wonders and miracles in setting people free from sin. Paul, in Romans 8:11, identifies the Holy Spirit as the agent of the Lord's resurrection. The Holy Spirit was active at every point in the life of Jesus. He alone empowered Christ for effective ministry.

In the final days of His earthly ministry, Jesus promised to send the Holy Spirit to His disciples (John 15). As Jesus once stood beside the disciples, now the Spirit would dwell within them. The Spirit's ministry would be one of instruction, support, help, protection, comfort and intercession. If the disciples hoped to fulfill Christ's ministry, they needed the Holy Spirit's presence in their lives.

Acts chapter 1 begins with the ascension story. It had been 50 days since the resurrection. Jesus gathered His disciples to give them final instructions "through the Holy Spirit." He expressly commanded them, "Do not leave Jerusalem, but wait for the gift my Father promised, which you have heard me speak about. For John baptized with water, but in a few days you will be baptized with the Holy Spirit" (Acts 1:4–5). He then said, "You will receive power when the Holy Spirit comes on you; and you will be my witnesses . . ." (Acts 1:8).

The implication is obvious. If the disciples ever hoped to fulfill the Lord's commands, they had to be Spirit-filled. Only after receiving His power could they go out to transform the world in Jesus' name. And that is precisely what happened. At Pentecost they were baptized in the Holy Spirit. Empowered by God, the disciples went from the upper room and revolutionized their world. Acts records dynamic church growth, as thousands upon thousands turned to Jesus Christ. This was a direct result of the Spirit-filled witness of the Lord's disciples. The Holy Spirit was actively present at every point of first century evangelism. So it must be for us today!

People in today's world have deep emotional and spiritual needs. Men and women hunger for security, acceptance, significance, identity and a genuine sense of belonging. Young people are turning to the occult in frightening numbers in a desperate search for transcendence. It is to this world that we are called and that we must minister the message of life in Christ. The only way for us to truly witness, meet real needs and do more than share objective truth is to walk in the power of the Holy Spirit.

Here are some specific ways the Holy Spirit works in evangelism. First, the Holy Spirit resides in the Christian witness, guiding and teaching him or her to live for Jesus. He develops fruit and gifts necessary for a person to be a child of God. The Spirit leads the Christian to go and share his or her faith in Christ. If sensitive to the Spirit, the Christian is guided to people who are open. He empowers him or her to communicate God's Word effectively. In addition, the Holy Spirit protects the witness from Satan's darts and equips the person to overcome the powers of darkness.

The ministry of the Holy Spirit also extends to unbelievers. He prepares them to hear and receive the gospel message. He convicts them of sin and rebellion, convincing them that life apart from God is futile. He reveals the glorious Savior through the testimony of the Christian witness. The Spirit leads people to repentance, regenerates their sinful hearts and indwells them when they confess Christ as Lord. Assurance of salvation, instruction in the Word and power for daily living are likewise linked to the Spirit's work. Finally, the fire of the Spirit in new Christians sends them out to witness to others.

And so I come back to my opening statement. Effective evangelism does not take place apart from the person and the work of the Holy Spirit. He is the essential fourth "P" of biblical evangelism. Christians must grow in their understanding of the Holy Spirit, praying for His leading in their lives and ministries. His presence makes the critical difference!

Chosen as His Messenger!

DAN WAS A WAYWARD YOUNG MAN in our community. He dropped out of high school in the 10th grade, primarily due to drug abuse. Other parents discouraged their teenagers from associating with Dan, making him even more antisocial and rebellious. His own parents seemed to have little time for or patience with him. They openly labeled Dan as the family black sheep. His hair was "too long," his clothes "too sloppy," his manner "too coarse" and his habits "too offensive." From nearly everyone's perspective, Dan was a lost cause. But Jesus Christ specializes in lost causes!

The Hahns were pillars of their local church. Tim was an elder and head of the Sunday school. Maggie was active in the women's fellowship group and taught the fourth grade Sunday school class. Together they raised two Christian sons—leaders in the local church youth group. Their eldest son, Jim, had known Dan since grade school. But in recent years he had had little contact with him. By God's design, they met one evening at a high school football game.

After the game, Jim invited Dan over for snacks and ping-pong. Though somewhat shocked by the invitation, Dan agreed. Deep inside he wondered if accepting was not a mistake. After all, parents were not particularly excited when he hung around.

But the Hahns were different. They seemed glad to see Dan and treated him with kindness. At the end of the evening, Tim and Maggie assured Dan that he was always welcome in their home. Soon Dan and Jim were regularly spending time together. Quite often Dan was included in family outings and was invited to special occasions in the Hahns' home. Rather than rejecting Dan, the entire family embraced and loved him just the way he was! His hair was still long, his clothes sloppy, his manner often coarse and his habits unacceptable. But beneath those outward signs of rebellion, they saw a tender young man begging for acceptance.

Maggie was particularly kind to Dan, causing him to frequently confide in her. She would listen as Dan poured out his heart, giving counsel when he was confused or discouraged. She regularly shared the message of God's love and salvation through Jesus Christ. At first Dan simply listened when Maggie spoke of forgiveness and everlasting life. But before long he began to ask questions—questions that betrayed a genuine interest and hunger. Knowing that Maggie was regularly witnessing to Dan, the entire family was praying as were people in their local church who knew about the situation.

The Hahns finally convinced Dan to attend a Sunday morning worship service with them. How well I remember seeing him enter the sanctuary with Tim and Maggie. His long, bushy hair and casual clothing caused some people to look twice, but for the most part, his arrival went unnoticed.

It was a normal worship service, not at all intended

to have an evangelistic appeal. To this day I cannot even remember the topic of my sermon. What I do remember, though, is the sight of Maggie and Dan kneeling at the altar after the service. During the final hymn, Dan made his way to the front with Maggie at his side for support. There, she counseled and prayed with him, and Dan surrendered his broken heart to the Lord Jesus Christ.

God radically transformed Dan's life, and he soon was involved in the life of our church. His zeal and enthusiasm for Christ were infectious; he just could not get enough. He wanted to learn everything he could about this new-found faith. Anyone and everyone who knew Dan made the same comment, "That's not the Dan we knew!" And they were right. "The old has gone, the new has come!" (2 Corinthians 5:17).

One day Dan came bursting into my office, obviously upset about something. I invited him to sit down and tell me what was on his mind. Dan shared that his life was filled with joy because of his new birth in Christ. He was excited to be part of God's family—thrilled to be set free from the brokenness of his past! But more recently he had looked back and remembered his old friends still in bondage to drugs, alcohol and rebellion. His heart began to ache for them, and Dan was desperate that they hear about Jesus. At that he jumped from the chair and said, "Pastor, you have to go with me! You must tell them about this new life I've received! You have to tell them that they can experience it too!"

Dan was not prepared for my response. "Dan, I'm not going with you!" He stood speechless for several moments, looking at me in disbelief. Recovering from the unexpected blow, he finally asked, "Why not? I don't understand."

"Dan," I said, "I'm not going because *God has chosen you* to tell them about salvation in Jesus Christ!"

God has chosen you!

This story illustrates a critical principle of evangelism. Every disciple of Jesus Christ has the privilege and the responsibility to spread the message of salvation. Witnessing is not the exclusive duty of professional Christians who work vocationally in church-related ministries. Witnessing is foundational to being a follower of Jesus Christ.

If you are a disciple, you are called to tell neighbors, friends, relatives and casual acquaintances the glorious gospel message. Maggie was called just as much as I am. Dan may have been a new believer, but he too was chosen. And so are you! You are an ambassador of Christ, called to reconcile lost men and women to Jesus. He has committed to you the message of salvation. God wants to make an appeal to lost men and women through you (2 Corinthians 5:16–21). It is critical that you understand and accept this basic responsibility of Christian discipleship.

Scripture overwhelmingly supports this principle. First, look at the example of Christ's followers. In John 1 we read that Andrew met Jesus by the Jordan where John was baptizing. Immediately he rushed to share the good news with his brother, Peter. Likewise, Philip found Nathanael and told him about Jesus. Excited about Christ, they did not keep the message to themselves but shared it with friends and relatives.

In John 4 we have the record of our Lord's meeting with the Samaritan woman. At Jacob's well she learned of the "living water" available in Jesus Christ. What was her response? She went back into town and told the people, "Come, see a man who told me everything I ever did," (verse 29). The people followed her and many believed in Jesus because of her testimony about Him. She had willingly shared the good news!

Examples like these are found throughout the gospels. These individuals were not professional Christians; they were everyday people transformed by the message of Christ—men and women just like you and me! They were redeemed people who shared the Living Water of Christ with friends and neighbors, common folks who told hungry people where to find Christ, the Living Bread.

Second, consider the teaching of Jesus on this subject. He emphatically instructed His followers to spread the gospel message. In Matthew 10 we read that Jesus sent out the Twelve, telling them to preach the message of the kingdom. Some may argue that this was because of their position as apostles. But this same admonition was given to 70 others, an account detailed in Luke 10. We also have the Lord's post-resurrection instructions, where He commissions His followers to make disciples. Promising the Holy Spirit's help, He commanded them to be His witnesses in Jerusalem, Judea, Samaria and to the ends of the earth.

These commands were not bound by space and time, exclusive instructions for the 12 disciples. They represent the calling of all Christ's followers, whether in the 1st or 21st century. We must be witnesses to His message of salvation. Through word and deed we are to obediently fulfill His commission, bearing witness to the truth.

Third, the Apostle Paul teaches that every Christian is to be part of reaching the world for Christ. Probably his clearest instruction is found in Second Corinthians, a letter written to every member of that local church. In chapter 5 he calls all believers ambassadors—a word that reflects the Christian's role as God's representative in society. As representatives, Paul instructs believers to serve as instruments of reconciliation. He wants believers to stand in the gap between Christ and lost men and women. By living and sharing the gospel, we link a broken world to the redeeming King.

Have you heard the story of Walter Vivian? He was an official of the Columbia Broadcasting Company. Columbia was to transmit King George's speech to the London Naval Conference in 1930. The story is told about how moments before the broadcast, Vivian discovered a severed communication line. There was not enough time to repair it and still broadcast the king's message. So Vivian, committed to getting the broadcast through, grabbed a wire in each hand to restore the current. He was shocked and severely burned, but by standing in the gap, the message was heard throughout the land.

King Jesus has a message that must be proclaimed! And every Christian is called to make sure that that message is heard. Men, women, teenagers and children can all stand in the gap. This means taking advantage of every opportunity to share the gospel with lost and broken people. Granted, most Christians either do not understand this, or choose to ignore Christ's command. But countless others are building the kingdom as faithful witnesses. These people have said yes to their calling and are changing the world because of it. Are you ready to do the same?

All are called to be witnesses

Before we move on, it will be helpful if we differentiate between an evangelist and a faithful witness. First Corinthians 12 tells us that the Holy Spirit determines what part a Christian will play in the body of Christ (verses 4–11). He determines this by giving a spiritual gift or gifts to use in the work of ministry. Scripture lists many such gifts in three primary chapters: Ephesians 4, Romans 12 and First Corinthians 12. The Bible tells us that every Christian has at least one such gift that is to be used within the context of Christ's body.

A spiritual gift can be defined as:

> A special attribute given by the Holy Spirit to every member of the Body of Christ according to God's grace for use within the context of the Body.[10]

Discovering one's spiritual gift or gifts is important. Why? Because it helps a person perceive God's call upon his or her life. In other words, spiritual gifts identify the area of ministry in which a person should invest the majority of his or her time—the area that God has especially equipped him or her for.

One spiritual gift the Bible lists is the ability to be

an evangelist (Ephesians 4:11). Some Christians are equipped by the Holy Spirit to be effective in communicating the gospel and leading people to Christ. For them evangelism comes more naturally, and their efforts are especially fruitful.

Spiritually gifted evangelists should spend the majority of their ministry time in outreach. Some people, like Billy Graham and Luis Palau, serve vocationally as evangelists. Others are pastors or missionaries who consisently lead people to Jesus Christ. But countless gifted evangelists are laypeople who minister in specific evangelism programs in their local church.

Possibly God has given you the gift of evangelism. Saying yes to the following questions would be a sign that you should at least investigate the possibility more intentionally.[11] Have you led others to Jesus Christ? Do you enjoy sharing your personal testimony with non-Christians? Are you concerned that every Christian share his or her faith on a regular basis? Are you comfortable building relationships with non-Christians as a way of leading them to Christ? Of all ministries in the local church, would evangelism be your personal preference for involvement?

Having recognized that there is a spiritual gift of evangelism, we have to assert that most people do not have it. In fact, in healthy, growing churches only about 10 percent of the congregation will evidence that gift.[12] Does that mean only these people should be trained to share their faith and lead people to Christ? *Absolutely not!*

Even though some people are specifically gifted as evangelists, *all* believers are called to be faithful witnesses. A believer's gifts may lead him or her to other ministries, like teaching, counseling or administration. But he or she is still called to be a witness for Jesus Christ. Every disciple should be ready and able to communicate the message of salvation to lost friends, neighbors and relatives. He or she must be prepared to rescue non-Christians from Satan's bondage. While gifted evangelists are God's regular army, all Christians are called to be His minutemen. Men and women need to be ready at any moment to share the good news that can set people free. This is what it means to be a faithful witness. Through word and deed, everyday Christians are announcing the gospel of Christ to their contacts in the non-Christian world. You do not need to ask if this means you. Just like Dan, Maggie and every other follower of Christ including me, *you are chosen!* You are chosen to communicate the greatest message the world will ever hear!

You must know the message

My conversation with Dan did not end with my announcing to him that he was chosen to tell his friends about Christ. He immediately asked, almost in a panic, "But what would I say?" Dan was putting his finger on the critical follow-up to accepting the role as Christ's ambassador. Believers must know the gospel message and know it well. Imagine a general engaged in a great battle against a powerful enemy. In the midst of the conflict he chooses a messenger to go to a battalion with instructions to attack. Before that soldier moves out, there is one important requirement. He must know the message! He must know it well and be able to

communicate it with clarity and passion. After all, it
is a matter of life and death.

You are Christ's ambassador! You are called to announce the good news to neighbors, friends and
relatives. Do you know the message of salvation?
Can you communicate it with clarity and passion?
Have you so familiarized yourself with the gospel
that you can proclaim it in such a way that people
will understand and respond? Are you ready to carry
this life and death message behind enemy lines? As a
disciple of Christ you have no option. You must
know and tell the gospel!

What exactly is the gospel message, this good news
that you must know and tell? At its most basic level,
it is the story about Jesus. That is, that He

> died for our sins and was raised from the dead,
> and that in consequence he reigns as Lord and
> Savior at God's right hand, and has authority
> both to command repentance and faith, and to
> bestow forgiveness of sins and the gift of the
> Spirit in all those who repent, believe and are
> baptized.[13]

As you can see from Pastor John Stott's definition,
the gospel message deals with several key issues: sin,
Christ's death and resurrection, His authority to forgive sins, repentance and faith. Knowledge of these
basic doctrines of the Christian faith is essential to
effective witnessing.

Obviously, to thoroughly understand salvation
themes, you should take Bible study seriously. After
all, the story of redemption runs throughout all of
Scripture, a scarlet thread from Genesis to Revelation. As God's faithful witness, you must grow in

knowledge and understanding of the whole counsel of God. This takes personal study and involvement in various Bible and Sunday school classes within the local church. By grounding yourself in the Old and New Testaments, you are able to relate the specific issues of the gospel to the whole of God's revelation. Such thorough-going inquiry into Scripture helps you fulfill the admonition of the Apostle Paul to Timothy: "Do your best to present yourself to God as one approved, a workman who does not need to be ashamed and who correctly handles the word of truth" (2 Timothy 2:15).

The gospel of Jesus Christ grows out of the complete revelation of God in the Bible. While you do not necessarily share the entire scope of God's redemptive plan, it is important that you have a solid, foundational understanding of His Word.

But at the practical level of witnessing, believers must be ready to share the more basic message of salvation through Jesus Christ—the basic message of God's love, our sin and the redemptive plan of Jesus. This salvation message can be best divided into four major headings: God's plan for life and abundance; the problem of sin; God's provision in Jesus Christ; the sinner's necessary response. If you can communicate the basic thrust of these four themes, you are ready to "announce" the gospel to your friends and neighbors.

God's plan for your life

Everywhere we look, we see people wrestling with problems. Not just the daily irritations of life, but deep, inner struggles. People of all ages are living with painful wounds that emotionally cripple. Victims of abuse and rejection, they build walls to hide behind and find protection. As a way of escaping pain they run to various forms of dependency. Other people live with an overwhelming sense of emptiness, questioning life's purpose and meaning. "Why am I here? Where did I come from? Where am I going?" Philosophic questions like these never end, bringing a sense of frustration and futility. The bottom line is clear: people are lost, broken and, for the most part, without a clue to finding peace in this world of confusion. It is not at all difficult to support this case, is it? Just look around.

But this was not God's plan. Instead of pain and frustration, God intended men and women to experience peace and abundance. In John 10 Jesus referred to Himself as the Good Shepherd who came to lead people to life and abundance. This life and abundance was God's desire from the foundation of creation. Consider Genesis 1. Two truths ring out repeatedly. God created everything, and everything He created was good. The biblical picture of paradise is most beautiful—a world where all creation was in harmony. Human beings were at one with God, in tune with each other and at peace within. Eden was truly a place of life and abundance!

There was one requirement to maintain harmony and blessedness in Eden—obedience. God reigned as King, and humanity was required to obey Him in all things. Out of obedience flowed abundance. God warned that disobedience would bring death. The tree of the knowledge of good and evil stood as the boundary of blessing. Adam and Eve were told to stay away from that tree, never to eat of its fruit. Faithfulness to this command would have ensured

harmony and peace in Eden—blessings through obedience! This was God's divine intention.

The problem of sin

If peace and abundance were God's plan, what
happened? Our world is no paradise, and brokenness has categorically replaced abundance. Why?
What went wrong?

Look again at John 10. While Jesus refers to Himself as the Good Shepherd, He likewise mentions a
thief—someone who has no intention of leading
people to life and abundance. Instead, he comes to
kill and destroy. Christ's reference again parallels
Genesis and the story of the Fall. As I have already
stated, God's standard was clear—obedience. But
Satan, that thief disguised as a serpent, tempted
Adam and Eve to do the thing God told them not to
do. He convinced them that disobedience would
bring blessing, not a curse.

Adam and Eve believed Satan and surrendered to
his temptation. In disobeying God, the harmony of
Eden became despair and disharmony. Adam and
Eve fell short of God's expectation and as a result
were separated from Him. All the blessings of obedience, life and abundance, came to an immediate
end. And ever since that day, sin and separation
have kept humankind in brokenness and bondage.
The sentence of death hangs over us all as an eternal
curse. What is the problem? Why do people live in
confusion and despair rather than peace and life?
The answer to both questions is the same. Human
beings are sinful and separated from God.

The Bible is clear at this point. Everyone is a sinner. ''For all have sinned and fall short of the glory

of God'' (Romans 3:23). To sin involves falling short of God's expectation. The Greek root of the word sin is *harmartia*. It is actually an archer's term, referring to arrows that do not hit their target. They miss the mark by falling short. What a powerful image of the human dilemma. People are separated from God because they fall short of obedience. They break His laws, which divorces them from the blessings of harmony with Him.

Men and women were created to have fellowship with God, but instead they live by their own rebellious self-will. People do things that are far short of His desire and standard. As a result they live in brokenness, unable to experience the abundance God intended. Instead of peace, people are confused and empty. Worst of all, sinful men and women will experience eternal separation from God in hell (Romans 6:23). God's plan is abundance, but humanity's problem is separation caused by sin.

God's provision in Jesus Christ

Sin and its destructive consequence is the bad news. Falling short of God's standard of obedience has robbed every person of life's blessings. Worst of all, people are absolutely helpless, unable to do anything about it. Sin stands as a barrier to God, separating people from His peace and abundance. On their own, they are hopelessly, eternally lost! Nothing they can do will right the wrong or erase the offense. Not good works, religion, philosophy, philanthropy or morality. Without God's help, all humanity is doomed.

God had every right to leave humanity in brokenness and despair. After all, it was humankind that

rebelled against Him. He was faithful to His promises, while men and women consistently rejected
Him. God could have turned His back on the entire
human race, sentencing us to eternal darkness and
death. But instead, out of His great mercy and love,
God sought to bring sinful men and women back to
Himself, back to His blessing and abundance, back
to His original plan.

Look again at Genesis 3. Adam and Eve openly
rebelled against God. Then they hid from God—a
sign of their separation from His love and blessing.
But in verse 9 we see evidence of God's deep grace
and mercy. Instead of rejecting Adam and Eve, He
sought them out. This is the first glimpse we have of
God's reconciling heart. In spite of our rebellion and
sin, the Heavenly Father wants to draw us back. He
longs to embrace sinners as His children once again.
The Apostle Paul wrote that God "wants all men to
be saved and to come to a knowledge of the truth"
(1 Timothy 2:4). Peter said that God is "not wanting
anyone to perish, but everyone to come to repentance" (2 Peter 3:9). While we can do nothing to save
ourselves, God's great love led Him to do everything. He provided a way.

The good news of salvation is this: "For God so
loved the world that he gave his one and only Son,
that whoever believes in him shall not perish but
have eternal life" (John 3:16). God loved us so much
that He sent His Son to be our Savior. Jesus came to
reconcile us to our Heavenly Father. Or, in His own
words, Jesus said, "I am the way and the truth and
the life. No one comes to the Father except through
me" (John 14:6). God made a marvelous provision
for us. He gave us Jesus.

What specifically did Jesus come to do for us? According to Scripture He came to pay for our sins. His death on Calvary's cross was on our behalf. At the price of His blood, Jesus provided both forgiveness and cleansing. He was our substitutionary sacrifice. Because Jesus paid for our sin on the cross, we can experience life as we were meant to experience it. The resurrection of Jesus is proof positive that God accepted His sacrificial death as sufficient. By Christ's death there is now a way of salvation.

Consider the following Scriptures that clearly communicate the meaning of Christ's death on the cross:

> When you were dead in sin . . . God made you alive with Christ. He forgave us all our sins, having cancelled the written code, with its regulations, that was against us . . .; he took it away, nailing it to the cross. (Colossians 2:13–14)

> For even the Son of Man did not come to be served, but to serve, and to give his life as a ransom for many. (Mark 10:45)

> But God demonstrates his own love for us in this: While we were still sinners, Christ died for us. (Romans 5:8)

> He himself bore our sins in his body on the tree. (1 Peter 2:24a)

> The blood of Jesus his Son, purifies us from all sin. (1 John 1:7b)

And then, to once again refer to the parallel in John 10 we read: "I am the good shepherd. The good shepherd lays down his life for the sheep" (verse 11).

What wondrous good news! God has made a provision for us. Every one of us, everywhere, struggling in brokenness, can be reconciled to God. We can find the abundance God intended from the beginning. Forgiveness and cleansing is provided for us all! How? Through Jesus Christ, God's Son. His death on Calvary was for our sins, making it possible for us to be reunited with God. Jesus is the way of salvation!

The necessary response

The gospel message does not end with the announcement that Jesus died for our sin. There is a fourth and critical element to the urgent message you are called to proclaim. We must individually respond to God's offer of salvation. It is not enough that God has provided Christ as our Redeemer. We must receive Jesus as Savior and Lord of our lives. Again, reflect on what the Bible declares.

> Yet to all who received him, to those who believed in his name, he gave the right to become children of God. (John 1:12)

> That if you confess with your mouth, ''Jesus is Lord,'' and believe in your heart that God raised him from the dead, you will be saved. (Romans 10:9)

> For it is by grace you have been saved, through faith—and this not from yourselves, it is the gift of God—not by works, so that no one can boast. (Ephesians 2:8-9)

> Here I am! I stand at the door and knock. If anyone hears my voice and opens the door, I

will come in and eat with him, and he with me.
(Revelation 3:20)

Each of these Scriptures tells us that a personal response is necessary. Salvation is God's lifeline, offered to people struggling in sin's treacherous storm.
But it does no good until it is trusted and embraced
personally. A drowning man is not saved simply because a lifeguard has tossed him a rope. Even if that
line is secure and able to save his life, it is powerless
until the struggling man reaches out to clutch it. So
it is with God's offer of salvation in Christ. We must
receive it!

The late David Watson, Anglican minister in England, used four words to clarify the steps we need to
take in receiving Christ: *turn, trust, take* and *thank*.[14]

Turn. We must turn from living life our own way to
living it for God. This is the step of repentance. We
say no to sin and yes to God. This must be a con-
scious choice in which we turn away from wrong
and turn to Christ.

Trust. Watson emphasizes two ways in which we
must trust Christ. First, we must trust that Christ
did die for us. Belief in Christ's sacrificial death is
essential. Second, we must trust Jesus as Lord. All of
our life is now under His authority. Obedience to
Him in every area of life is essential, just as it was in
Eden. Christ must be on the throne as Lord of all.
Otherwise, He is not Lord at all. While it is difficult
to understand all that Christ's Lordship means, it is
a nonnegotiable requirement of Christian discipleship.

Take. Salvation is a free gift of eternal life through
Jesus Christ. As Watson says, ''God waits for me to

stretch out my empty hands and take from Him this most valuable gift that I could ever have."[15] We do this by faith, and God's Holy Spirit regenerates our hearts. We are born anew into God's forever family.

Thank. Again Watson says, "As with so many aspects of life, it is only when we act as though something were true that it ever becomes true."[16] Thanking Christ is an active way of taking Him at His word. We must confess the claims of Scripture as a way of making this confession the conviction of our hearts.

The gospel of Jesus Christ is the greatest message the world has ever heard. And all of us are given the privilege of announcing this news everywhere, every day. The four-fold outline presented here is a helpful way to embrace the gospel message and to communicate it clearly. Familiarizing yourself with the four steps, and with the related Scriptures, will prepare you to share the good news. Remember, *you are chosen to spread His message.*

As I close this chapter, consider a familiar fable that illustrates the Lord's call upon our lives.

When Jesus returned to heaven following the ascension, the angels were thrilled to see Him. One angel asked the returned Christ a question. "What plan do you have to continue Your work on earth?" Immediately the Lord said, "It is in the hands of my followers." Another angel asked, "But what if they fail? What if they do not do what you asked?" Again Jesus quickly responded, "I have no other plan."

Why Should I Get Involved?

P ROBABLY LIKE MANY OF YOU, I was a post World War 2 baby. One implication of this special status was growing up listening to countless "war stories." My father, grandfather and father-in-law each served in the U.S. armed forces during the war years. Tales of basic training, life on a Pacific island and bombing missions over Germany were (and still are) part of oral tradition in our family. And rightly so. The Second World War was a critical chapter in history, involving great sacrifices for millions of people.

I have always found it interesting that members of my family *enlisted* for wartime service. After all, they were not professional soldiers. My father and grandfather were coal miners and my father-in-law, a company clerk. Their vocations did not prepare them for the rigors of war. Yet, when the need arose, they willingly joined the armed forces to serve the cause of freedom.

Ask these men why they went, and the answers are the same—the country needed them. The conflict was too great to be fought by professional soldiers alone. Every able-bodied person was asked to help, asked to do whatever he or she could. And so, after only "basic training," they joined countless other

G.I.s for wartime service. Why did they get involved? They felt it was their duty. They went because they were needed in that urgent hour. History records that those "irregulars" meant the difference between victory and defeat.

The Scriptures tell us that there is a great war raging all about. "For our struggle is not against flesh and blood, but against the rulers, against the authorities, against the powers of this dark world and against the spiritual forces of evil in the heavenly realms" (Ephesians 6:12). This war is global in scope, and the object is the hearts of men and women. The hour is late, a time when all God's people must do their part. Billions of people are held in spiritual bondage, doomed to eternal darkness, prisoners of Satan's tyranny. Christians everywhere are needed as God's army does battle against the forces of wickedness.

Unfortunately, most Christians feel the battle is to be fought by professionals only. They think evangelism is solely the obligation of ministers and missionaries. While 99 percent of the church is made up of laypeople, 95 percent of American church members have never led a single person to Jesus Christ.[17] It is as if God's "G.I.s" decided to stay home and not get involved. Because of this attitude, the church is not advancing against the enemy as it could or should.

Winning this world for Christ demands total commitment and involvement. It will take sacrificial service from ministers, missionaries *and* laypeople. Granted, mobilizing an otherwise inactive army is no small task. But it must be done. It begins by understanding the various reasons why the average

Christian should get involved. Why should you be motivated to serve in God's army of witnesses? That is the primary focus of this chapter.

Obedience

The true test of Christian discipleship is obedience. Scripture makes this clear. In the Gospel of John we have the account of Jesus' teaching in the upper room. Our Lord gathered with His disciples for one final passover celebration. Afterward, the cross. During those final hours, Jesus taught the Twelve those "last things" so important once He was gone. He told them of love and servanthood, the hatred of the world and the sending of the Comforter. And Jesus reminded them of the central standard of discipleship—obedience.

> If you love me, you will obey what I command. (John 14:15)

> Whoever has my commands and obeys them, he is the one who loves me. (John 14:21a)

> If you obey my commands, you will remain in my love. (John 15:10a)

> You are my friends if you do what I command. (John 15:14)

Jesus linked obedience to love. He evaluated the love of His followers by more than emotion and sentiment. He measured it by obedience. If they loved Christ, they would obey Him. Jesus showed His love for God by obedience and expected the same of His disciples.

The obedience theme runs from Genesis to Revelation. Certainly it was a fundamental theme in the Old Testament record, beginning with the story of creation. The blessings of Eden were contingent on obedience. Likewise, during the exodus, obedience was the obligation of God's covenant people. Consider these words in Deuteronomy:

> Hear now, O Israel, the decrees and laws I am about to teach you. Follow them so that you may live and may go in and take possession of the land that the Lord, the God of your fathers, is giving you. Do not add to what I command you and do not subtract from it, but keep the commands of the Lord your God that I give you. (4:1-2)

As the Israelites finally approached Canaan, God restated His standard to Joshua (Joshua 1). He commanded him to obey all the Law, not turning from it to the right or to the left. Joshua's obedience would result in promised abundance.

God rejected Saul as king over Israel because he disobeyed. The Lord had told Saul to go up against the Amalekites in battle. He was instructed to destroy everything belonging to that pagan people. But after the battle, Saul spared all the best sheep and cattle. This grieved God and greatly troubled the prophet Samuel. Samuel went to meet Saul and rebuked him for not following the Lord's instructions. Saul, trying to justify his disobedience, said he only spared them for sacrifice to the Lord. Samuel's reply stands as a reminder to God's people for all time: "Does the Lord delight in burnt offerings and sacrifices / as much as in obeying the voice of the Lord? / To obey is better than sacrifice" (1 Samuel 15:22).

Why so much time lifting the standard of obedience? There are two reasons. First, because Christianity in the United States today is heavily influenced by easy-believism. Churches are filled with people who want all the benefits of salvation without surrendering to its requirements. Jesus has become a "sugar daddy" in the sky. People want His forgiveness, protection, provision and everlasting life, yet they ignore repentance, suffering, sacrifice and the cross. Too many people are saying yes to salvation but no to His commands.

Christian social activist Jim Wallis says, "the great tragedy of modern evangelism is in calling many to belief but few to obedience."[18] People rush to accept Christ as Savior, yet fail to submit to His Lordship in their lives. This results in an impossible marriage of Christianity and paganism. Christo-pagans want the safety of Christ's salvation while living their day-to-day lives by their own worldly standards. But such a wedding is not made in heaven and leads only to disaster.

There is no discipleship divorced from obedience. The two go hand in hand. German martyr Dietrich Bonhoeffer forcefully championed this concept in his classic work, *The Cost of Discipleship*. Writing on the balance between grace and obedience he stated:

> "Only those who believe obey" is what we say to that part of a believer's soul which obeys, and "only those who obey believe" is what we say to that part of the soul of the obedient which believes.[19]

Belief and obedience are married. One without

the other results in either cheap grace or works-righteousness. Christ's grace-redeemed disciples are His obedient servants. This is the biblical standard. This is the marriage that gives birth to true Christlike service and discipleship.

There is a second reason for lifting up the standard of obedience. And for this discussion on evangelism it is the primary reason for mentioning the issue. Obedience is the most basic motivation for communicating the gospel of Jesus Christ. Anyone who asks, "Why should I get involved in evangelism?" can be answered in one word—obedience.

Our Lord made it clear that He wanted all people to hear the good news of salvation. He desired that everyone know, regardless of age, class, race, language, geographic region or cultural diversity. Jesus translated His concern into a command for every disciple of all time. Through what has become known as the Great Commission, He directed His followers to "make disciples." This commission was not a suggestion to a few professional Christians. It is Christ's command for you, for me, for His church.

The Great Commission of Jesus is recorded five times in Scripture—Matthew 28:18-20, Mark 16:15, Luke 24:33-39, John 20:21 and Acts 1:7-8. It is interesting that this command was the first and last instruction He gave following the resurrection. It certainly amplifies the importance of Christ's mandate. Jesus wanted His followers to be crystal clear at this point. They—we—would be responsible for spreading the message of salvation throughout the world. Reconciliation was now possible, and Christ commanded His followers to tell the good news.

The most familiar and complete expression of the

Great Commission is recorded in the Gospel of Matthew:

> All authority in heaven and on earth has been given to me. Therefore go and make disciples of all nations, baptizing them in the name of the Father and of the Son and of the Holy Spirit, and teaching them to obey everything I have commanded you. And surely I am with you always, to the very end of the age. (28:18–20)

Reading this leaves little question about the believer's responsibility toward evangelism and outreach. The church is under orders to make disciples. This is, in fact, the imperative of the Great Commission. Why the Lord chose to place such a responsibility in our hands is not clear. But the fact that He did is undeniable.

Evangelical scholar J.I. Packer writes,

> Evangelism is the inalienable responsibility of every Christian community and every Christian man. We are all under orders to devote ourselves to spreading the good news. . . . This is a responsibility that cannot be shrugged off.[20]

Through the power of the Holy Spirit, disciples are called to witness to every people-group on earth. The church of Christ moves out under these orders, marching on to obediently accomplish the Lord's command. Not one Christian has the luxury to sit by uninvolved.

So you see, your commitment to evangelism begins with obedience. We have established that true disciples follow the Lord's instructions. As His servant, you have already said yes to that condition. Spreading the good news is a command from the Lord. You must be involved in outreach out of obedience to the risen Christ. Are you involved? You should be!

Love For God

It was a hot Sunday evening at Ft. Bragg, North Carolina. The date was September 22, 1957. Lt. John Stevey was on his first assignment as an Army chaplain, the fulfillment of years of hard work and preparation. He had only been at Ft. Bragg a few days. This was his first Sunday evening service.

These were good days for John, and in his heart he anticipated even greater times to come. The only disappointment was that his lovely wife Joan was not yet with him. But in truth, that was OK, too, for she was back in Washington, Pennsylvania, soon to deliver their first baby. Any day now, John expected to get the call that began with the words, "Congratulations, Dad!"

As the service ended, John received a note instructing him to call home. With great excitement he dialed Washington, fully expecting to hear the news of the stork's arrival. The voice at the other end of the phone line confirmed that Joan had given birth to a baby boy. But the news was not at all good. The birth was traumatic, and John was being summoned home. The doctor, who had performed mouth to mouth resuscitation on the baby for over 20 minutes, did not expect this newborn baby to live through the night.

John arrived at the hospital not knowing what to expect. Had Joel—the name they selected ahead of time for a boy baby—died before he could see him? Was Joan okay? Were they prepared to face whatever happened? These questions ate at his soul as he hurried to the maternity ward. Before entering Joan's room he paused to yet again place everything in the hands of the Lord. And he prayed for strength.

John's reunion with Joan was filled with emotion. There was joy, sorrow, fear, trust, tears and words of support. And, of course, the most powerful force of all was at work—love! Their love for God and for each other was unquestionable. Deep inside they somehow believed that the power of their two loves would see them through. No matter how dark the night, love would shine forth and point the way to a new day.

Joel had not died as John had feared. In fact, the doctor, amazed at the baby's progress, gave some hope that he was coming "out of the woods." But this good news was wrapped in a terrible reality. Joel was severely brain-damaged and, according to the physician, would exist all his days as a "vegetable." He would never walk or talk, and never respond to them in any way. At best, Joel would be institutionalized for his entire life.

This news hit hard. When John saw his son, Joel was weak, connected to monitors and tubes for life support. Yet, John and Joan loved him. They loved Joel with the same love they felt for God and for each other—a love that gave hope in this storm, and confidence for tomorrow. No matter what it would take, regardless of the cost, Joel would receive all that their love could afford.

As John looked through the glass at Joel, he was aware of a happy father standing beside him, also looking at the newborns. Seeing Joel, the man commented, "Too bad about that little guy, isn't it?"

"Oh, it's okay," John responded. "You see, he's mine, and he'll do just fine." That was a father's love speaking out confidence and hope for his wounded son!

John, Joan and Joel Stevey are friends of mine. They are part of our seminary community where John is dean of students. Yes, Joel is still handicapped, unable to walk or talk. But he is one of the most delightful, intelligent, loving young men I know. His mother and dad never institutionalized him. Instead, they prayed and struggled with him through all the hard times. Love helped them keep Joel home when others said to send him away. Love led them to invest in Joel's education, when people thought it fruitless and ill-advised. Love motivated John to retire from chaplaincy early so Joel could have stability and the chance at a career. Love moves his parents to daily care for all his personal needs. And love keeps Mom and Dad speaking with pride about their courageous son.

Joel is 31 now. Despite all prognostications, he is a productive computer programmer for a local industrial firm. Though he cannot speak, Joel communicates by using a specially designed computer that is attached to his wheelchair. He has won national awards, been a leader in a handicapped Boy Scout patrol and published an article in a nationwide newsletter. Joel is a positive, upbeat young man, loved by many in our community. He is living proof that love makes a difference.

I asked John if they have a family verse.

"Not a verse, a chapter!" he said. And of course it is First Corinthians 13!

The Stevey's story illustrates the power of love.

Love is life's greatest motivator, leading people to go to any length to express its commitment. Of course, the greatest example of love's commitment is that of Jesus. He willingly left glory to become one of us. Born in the humblest circumstances, He grew up in poverty and anonymity. His earthly ministry was only three years in length, and for the most part, He was rejected by the religious community. Though He came proclaiming reconciliation and peace, He experienced great hatred and animosity. At the end He was abandoned by even His closest followers. Jesus was betrayed, framed in a mock trial, cruelly tortured and ultimately killed by one of the most painful methods ever devised by man. Even in death, crowds mocked and jeered, a tragic farewell from a lost and broken world. At any time He could have called for divine intervention. But Jesus did not; He endured the pain without bitterness or malice.

Why? What force lay behind our Lord's submission to such unjust treatment? It was the power that upholds the universe—the power of love. This is love that goes far beyond shallow sentimentality. Jesus Christ was motivated by the purest love known to man—the quality of love reflected in First Corinthians 13. It is the kind of love that moves a person to endure anything for the one concerned, the kind of love that sent the Son of God to die so that sinful people can be set free. Why did Christ endure the cross, the shame, the rejection? He was motivated by love—a love that was proven by actions, a love that cost Him everything.

That brings us again to this matter of evangelism. Why should you or I get involved? By now the answer is obvious. We Christians share our faith in response to God's grace and redeeming love. Jesus was moved by love to climb Calvary and die on a cross for us. Our love should send us willingly into the world to share His message of reconciliation and everlasting life. If we love Him, we will gladly pay the price of evangelism.

Micheal Green, Anglican pastor and author, states that such a sense of love motivated the early church. He wrote:

> These men did not spread their message because it was advisable for them to do so, nor because it was the socially responsible thing to do. They did not do it primarily for humanitarian or agathistic utilitarian reasons. They did it because of the overwhelming experience of the love of God which they had received through Jesus Christ.[21]

Believers today are still experiencing God's great love. And in response, His people should carry the good news around the globe. Do you love God? If so, then I'm sure you want to proclaim that message to others.

The lostness of humanity

People who live and die without a personal relationship with the Lord Jesus Christ are lost. They are lost now, and they are lost for all eternity. Granted, this is a harsh reality. Yet it is a basic tenet of the Christian faith. This scriptural principle holds true for relatives who are not Christians as much as for people we do not even know. It relates not only to primitive tribesmen in distant lands but to the unbelieving neighbor who lives next door. Anyone and everyone who has not surrendered to the Lordship of Christ is living under the shadow of eternal death. Lost!

The Bible is clear on this point. Throughout the pages of Scripture, there are warnings of judgment for those who chose to live sinfully. Consider just these passages taken from the New Testament:

> I say to you that many will come from the east and the west, and will take their places at the feast with Abraham, Isaac and Jacob in the kingdom of heaven. But the subjects of the kingdom will be thrown outside, into the darkness, where there will be weeping and gnashing of teeth. (Matthew 8:11–12)

> Do not be afraid of those who kill the body but cannot kill the soul. Rather, be afraid of the One who can destroy both soul and body in hell. (Matthew 10:28)

> As the weeds are pulled up and burned in the fire, so it will be at the end of the age. The Son of Man will send out his angels, and they will weed out of his kingdom everything that causes sin and all who do evil. They will throw them into the fiery furnace, where there will be weeping and gnashing of teeth. (Matthew 13:40–42)

> The wrath of God is being revealed from heaven against all the godlessness and wickedness of men who suppress the truth by their wickedness. (Romans 1:18)

> For the wages of sin is death, but the gift of God

is eternal life in Christ Jesus our Lord. (Romans 6:23)

Do you not know that the wicked will not inherit the kingdom of God? (1 Corinthians 6:9a)

Then I saw a great white throne and him who was seated on it. Earth and sky fled from his presence, and there was no place for them. And I saw the dead, great and small, standing before the throne, and books were opened. Another book was opened, which is the book of life. The dead were judged according to what they had done as recorded in the books. The sea gave up the dead that were in it, and death and Hades gave up the dead that were in them, and each person was judged according to what he had done. Then death and Hades were thrown into the lake of fire. The lake of fire is the second death. If anyone's name was not found written in the book of life, he was thrown into the lake of fire. (Revelation 20:11–15)

The separation and damnation of those who refuse Christ the Savior is sure and awesome. Certainly Scripture abounds with passages that speak of God's love, mercy, grace, forgiveness and blessing. These texts give testimony to a patient, benevolent Creator who would willingly give eternal life to all. But the requirement of His justice demands that salvation rest upon the Savior, Jesus Christ. Anyone living *or* dying apart from Him is lost. C. Peter Wagner puts it this way:

What do you mean by lost? Lost materially and socially? Yes. Lost physically? Yes. Lost spiritually? Yes, and this is the most serious of all since it carries the possibility that man will be separated from God for eternity in hell. . . . Because of sin, every man and every woman is headed for hell, but no one needs to arrive there. The difference between those who arrive and those who do not is Jesus Christ. Those who confess the Lord Jesus and believe in their hearts that God raised Him from the dead will be saved (Romans 10:9). Those who don't, will not.[22]

Think about this for a moment. Consider the devastating consequence of living and dying without Christ. And remember this: most people alive today are headed for just such a fate! Apathy and ignorance have kept them from hearing the glorious message of salvation in Jesus. Every single day tens of thousands die, hurled into a dark, destructive, Godless eternity. Many of these lost men and women are relatives, friends and neighbors. Our communities are populated by people who are condemned to eternal judgment. The lost are in every village, town, city and nation around the world.

The telling question is this, *Do you care?* As a Christian you have the message that can save lost men and women—the message that can set relatives, neighbors and friends free forever and ever. Your words of Christ can turn them from darkness to light, from eternal death to everlasting life. Are you reaching out? Will you throw them the lifeline of the gospel? Are you committed to being a witness to them?

If we possess even the slightest degree of human kindness, we should be gripped with concern for the

lost. There should burn within us a desire to reconcile condemned men and women with Jesus Christ.
Leighton Ford tells the story of a prisoner's conversation with a visiting chaplain. The chaplain had
shared the message of salvation with this man. The
prisoner responded, "So you really believe what you
say, chaplain? If I believed your gospel was true, I
would travel across England on broken glass to tell
men about it."[23]

God will never ask us to crawl across England on
broken glass. But He has commanded that we share
the message of salvation. If we really believe that
people are lost, we should willingly witness regardless of the cost. Knowing what faces those who are
lost without Christ, we should eagerly do our part in
God's rescue operation.

The full impact of this biblical truth hit me one
day as I traveled with my infant son. At the time, I
was pastor of a small-town church in southwestern
Pennsylvania. I was making a trip with Aaron, head-
ing to my parents' home 45 miles away. Along the
way I began to consider the fact that my grandmother had never been in church. Deep inside I
knew I should witness to her, yet I always found it
somewhat intimidating. But this time God flashed
before me the awesome reality of eternity apart from
Him. Thoughts of darkness, loneliness, despair and
eternal agony filled my mind. And then came this
piercing thought: my grandmother would surely
face it all! She was without Christ. She was lost!

Suddenly, apprehension was replaced with a sense
of urgency. I simply had to share the gospel of Christ
before she stepped into eternity. Aaron and I headed
for Grandma's immediately, praying for an open

door and a sensitive heart. It was indeed a divine appointment. Within minutes I had a perfect opportunity. As I shared the message of salvation, my grandmother commented, "I've waited all my life to hear this. How can I be born again?"

Picture in your mind those loved ones and acquaintances of yours who do not know Jesus Christ. If they were to die today, they would certainly face God's judgment and hell. Yet, you have the message of eternal life in Christ Jesus. If they hear and respond to that good news, they will be saved from everlasting death. Do you care? Will you pray for an open door? Do you accept God's call upon your life to tell them?

The power of the Holy Spirit

Our discussion of motivating factors in evangelism brings us finally to the greatest motivator of all—the Holy Spirit of God. Our Lord commanded the apostles to make disciples of all people. As discussed earlier, His command became the church's Great Commission. Interestingly, on the day of Christ's ascension, He added an all-important element to His instructions. While making His desire for world evangelization clear, Jesus told His followers to wait. "Do not leave Jerusalem, but wait for the gift my Father promised, which you have heard me speak about. For John baptized with water, but in a few days you will be baptized with the Holy Spirit" (Acts 1:4-5).

Jesus knew that evangelism was a spiritual matter that would demand Holy Spirit power. So He told the disciples to go to Jerusalem and wait for the Spirit. Even though their instructions to win the world were clear, they were to do nothing until He came. The Holy Spirit would be their helper in ministry. He would guide them to receptive people, anoint their preaching, equip them with miracle power and prepare hearts to receive the message. Most of all, the Holy Spirit would motivate Christ's followers to be His witnesses in the world.

Jesus Himself revealed the Spirit's role as motivator. He said, "But you will receive power when the Holy Spirit comes on you; and you will be my witnesses in Jerusalem, and in all Judea and Samaria, and to the ends of the earth" (Acts 1:8). Notice the two important ingredients in our Lord's statement. First, He confidently promised that the Holy Spirit would come. Second, He revealed what would happen once the Spirit gave His followers power. They would be Christ's witnesses everywhere. Jesus here shows us an almost cause-and-effect relationship between receiving the Spirit and sharing the gospel of salvation. In other words, when the Holy Spirit infills a person, he or she will be moved to witness.

Even a quick reading of Acts reveals that the Holy Spirit was the prime mover in the spread of early Christianity. The disciples obeyed Jesus and waited in almost constant prayer for 10 days in that Jerusalem upper room.

Suddenly, on the day of Pentecost, the Holy Spirit filled the entire house where they were sitting. He anointed each one of them with power (Acts 2). Immediately they spilled into the streets where they miraculously spoke in languages they had never learned. Visitors from surrounding nations were amazed as they listened to Christ's followers declare the wonders of God.

Peter then fearlessly preached a powerful sermon to everyone (Acts 2:14–40), in which he announced Jesus as the Christ. He called people to repentance, and on that day over 3,000 men became Christians. Remember, this was Peter! Peter, who only weeks earlier had denied Christ. Peter, who fearfully cursed and hid when a mere servant girl asked if he followed Jesus. Peter, who wept bitterly when the rooster crowed, reminding him of the Lord's prediction. But now, filled with the Holy Spirit, he witnessed boldly, inviting people to receive the Lord Jesus.

Throughout the book of Acts, we read of the Holy Spirit's motivating presence in the lives of Christ's followers. He empowered the disciples to speak boldly the word of truth. Even in the face of persecution and death, they went on proclaiming the message of salvation. Moved by the Holy Spirit, Christians fanned out across the Mediterranean, carrying the good news of salvation. Under the Spirit's leadership, the church grew, within three decades after Christ, from a handful of followers to tens of thousands. Just as Jesus said, they did receive power and they were His witnesses to the ends of the earth.

In *I Believe in the Holy Spirit*, Anglican pastor Micheal Green wrote,

[The Holy Spirit] was the leader of the whole Christian outreach as well as its energizing power. The church was only effective when it . . . followed the Spirit. It is the Spirit who energizes the evangelism of the church and drives its often unwilling members into the task for which God laid His hand on them—mission.[24]

Most Christians, we readily recognize, are unwilling to get involved in evangelism. When asked why, responses are generally the same. Some people say, "I don't know how." Others confess that a combination of fear and pride holds them back. Still others, if they were honest enough to admit it, are simply apathetic and indifferent. Many church members feel evangelism is a job for the specialist, not the everyday Christian. Certainly these negative factors keep countless believers silent and inactive. But the Holy Spirit can overcome all apprehension if you have an open, willing heart.

If you hunger for His presence and power, you can move beyond fear to faithfulness. You can be filled with Spirit power and become an effective witness. Like the disciples, you can be directed to receptive people by the Holy Spirit. And with His gentle guidance, you can share the glorious account of Christ's saving work on Calvary. The work of the Holy Spirit, as it relates specifically to spiritual power, will be discussed more in chapter 5.

Before reading this chapter you may have asked, "Why should I get involved in evangelism?" But if you are truthful, you cannot ask that anymore. As God's mighty army marches out to rescue men and women from Satan's death, you must be in the ranks. Witnessing is a matter of obedience! It is your willing response to God's all-redeeming love! You share your faith because you care about the lost and want to see them saved! Filled with the Holy Spirit, you can go out into the streets to tell neighbors, friends and relatives of new life in Christ!

Going Deeper with Christ

FOR SEVERAL YEARS I PASTORED a small congregation in rural Pennsylvania. We lived in a tiny community called Amity, which boasted of two churches, one general store, a firehouse and a post office. It was a picturesque settlement, surrounded by lovely farmlands and forests. The people of Amity were warm, humble folk, and they received us with love and affection. It was a great place to begin ministry, and Cheryl and I look back to those years with fond memories.

Having been accustomed to the suburbs, life in a rural village was quite different for us. One change we had not anticipated had to do with our water supply. We were used to city water systems, but in Amity, that was unavailable. Each home, including ours, had a well that was fed from an underground spring. Our water came from the well, brought into the house through a pump in the basement. It was a real novelty to us, and best of all, it was free!

Cheryl, being more cautious than I, was concerned that the well water was safe. After all, she was pregnant and wanted only the best for our baby. Everyone in the community said the water was fine, bragging that it was the best in the area. Cheryl, however, was unsatisfied and wanted a more objective appraisal. A water sampling was sent to a laboratory in a nearby town. Everyone was shocked and embarrassed when the report came back reading, "This water is unfit even for bathing."

The problem with the water was twofold. First, the well was not drilled deep enough. As a result, run off was seeping in, carrying bacteria from fertilizers and other debris. Second, the system was old, which meant the pipes and the filter were bad. Instead of keeping the water pure, they only contributed to the problem. To correct the situation, we had to renew the system and dig much deeper to reach a pure spring.

This incident speaks volumes to Christian life and service. In many ways a commitment to evangelism is a commitment to dispense Living Water. This Living Water comes through the Holy Spirit, a gift of the Lord to all who believe. Like an underground spring, the Water of Life is to well up within and nourish our lives. It should then flow out to others as an invitation to Christian discipleship. This is what Christ spoke of when He confronted the Samaritan woman and offered her the Water that would satisfy forever and ever.

Unfortunately, many Christians are unable to offer Living Water to the lost. Why? Because they lack depth in their relationship with Christ. Their experience of Jesus is shallow and polluted by worldly, un-Christian lifestyles. While trusting Christ for salvation, believers often do not grow in their daily walk with Him. They fail to regularly attend church, study Scripture, pray and fellowship with other Christians. As a result, shallow commitment keeps them from experiencing the Spirit's overflow. Such Christians struggle with their faith, and ultimately have little to offer others.

Effective evangelism demands a personal commitment to spiritual growth. A Christian's relationship to Christ must go deeper and deeper, reaching for the Spirit's overflow. This requires regular disciplines and commitments that draw him or her closer to the Lord Jesus. Preparation in evangelism begins here, developing quality devotion to our Lord that serves as the source of life and witness.

Such basic commitments will be the focus of this chapter. Together we will explore several foundational disciplines that lead to spiritual depth and maturity. Then, by developing our inner lives, we can grow strong in Christ and effectively share the Living Water with those thirsting for everlasting life.

Biblical priorities

Developing inner depth begins with establishing clear biblical priorities. We live in a busy, fast-paced world, where more and more demands are made upon our time. We often lament that there are not enough hours in a day. Busy schedules push areas of Christian commitment and development to the background. Many of the disciplines we will discuss never get developed. Much like the thorns Jesus spoke of in the parable of the sower, busy schedules begin to choke out the fruit of Christ's presence within. The only way to combat this is by establishing certain nonnegotiable commitments to spiritual development and growth.

Ray Ortlund, founder of Renewal Ministries, has

suggested that a balanced order of priorities is built upon three commitments:

Commitment to Christ
Commitment to the body of Christ
Commitment to the work of Christ in the world[25]

Priority one—commitment to Christ—means that Jesus comes first! He is to be the ruling passion and principal of our lives. No matter what else we are about, knowing and loving Him should be top priority. Time must be invested in developing our walk with the Lord. We must worship Him, study His Word, pray to Him and regularly fellowship with His people. Daily times of personal devotion and meditation are a must. This is foundational to spiritual health and depth, and it is the only way to develop and maintain a vital relationship with the Lord.

It is not news that most Christians have difficulty maintaining a consistent devotional time with the Lord. They may accept the principle that Jesus comes first, but their daily practice of this principle is weak or nonexistent. If this is true for you, consider these suggestions:

1. Surrender your weakness and inability in this area to the Lord. Confess ''I can't, but You can.'' If we believe, the Lord will draw us to Himself with a new hunger and zeal.
2. Keep the goal of your devotional time clear. Having a quiet time is not an end in itself, a task to check off when completed. The goal of devotions is devotion to Christ. It is meant to draw you into deeper fellowship with Him.
3. Choose your best time for devotions. We

often hear of saints who arose at 3:00 a.m. for prayer and study. Do not superimpose that schedule on your life. Evaluate the best time in your day and set that aside for Him.

4. Choose a quiet place. Distractions hinder quality time with the Lord. Seek a secluded place where His voice can be heard in prayer, reading and reflection. Possibly several spots can be identified that will add variety to your schedule.

5. Have a basic structure to your quiet time. This should include worship, prayer, Scripture and devotional reading. It is best to focus on a particular theme or book of the Bible. Numerous devotional guides are available for structuring your time.

6. Find a Christian brother or sister who will covenant to hold you accountable. All of us are more consistent when someone is committed to supporting and encouraging us. By developing such a relationship, you are better motivated to faithfully spend quality time before the Lord.

7. Learn to carry your devotion into the remainder of your day. Keep your focus on Jesus; carry Scripture cards to memorize, and pray in the empty moments of the day. Your quiet time then becomes a daily focus on Christ that lasts throughout the day.

I hope these guidelines will lead you into a consistent, quality walk with Christ. They are a practical way to keep Jesus as first priority in your life.

Priority two—commitment to the body of Christ—builds upon the practice of keeping Jesus first. It is the second nonnegotiable principle of spiritual depth and health. There is no New Testament evidence suggesting that God intends Christians to live and minister in isolation from each other. The Word emphasizes the unity and interrelationship of Christ's followers. In Acts 2, Peter preached a salvation message and 3,000 people believed. Notice what these new converts did (verses 41–47). They gathered regularly for teaching, worship, prayer and fellowship. In addition, they regularly ate together, shared resources and continually praised God. Far from a picture of isolation, the early Christians bonded together.

Our Lord began His earthly ministry proclaiming the gospel of the kingdom (Mark 1:15). Immediately Jesus proceeded to gather followers. These men grew strong in Him, grew together as brothers and eventually moved out into the world to proclaim His gospel. And they served as the nucleus for the church Christ promised to build (Matthew 16:13–18).

The word "church," translated from the Greek, is *ecclesia*. It fundamentally means, "those who have been called out." David Watson, in his book *I Believe in the Church*, provides helpful insights into the New Testament use of the word *ecclesia*. He wrote:

> First, it is used of the universal church, the entire company of believers, both living and dead. . . . Second, it is often used of a particular local church, such as the church at Cenchreae, Corinth, Thessalonica, or Laodicea. Third, it can mean the actual assembly of believers in any place as they meet together for worship. Fourth,

it can apply to a small house church, the regular meeting place for a small group of believers in any one town or city. However, whatever the size, it always speaks of the coming together of God's people in answer to His call, in order to meet with God in the company of each other and to meet each other in the presence of God.[26]

Notice the emphasis on believers coming together, assembling in the presence of God. The word clearly implies unity, bonding and fellowship in Christ.

The Apostle Paul likewise emphasizes the corporate nature of the church. In Ephesians 4 he urges unity and oneness among all believers. In verses 15 and 16 he likens the church to a body, with Christ as the Head. All parts of the body (Christians) are joined together, growing in love. In First Corinthians 12 he further develops the metaphor "body of Christ." Paul tells us that the church, made up of different people, is like many parts of one body, diverse yet united. Each person serves Christ, the Head, and supports, encourages and strengthens the other parts of His Body.

The bottom line of priority two is simply this: It is true that Christ is top priority in our lives, but the second most important commitment is to His church. Christians need one another to grow in Christ, stand strong against the enemy and reconcile this world to God. In practical terms, that means Christians must be active members of a local church. Spiritual health hinges in part on such a commitment. Believers need to worship together, learn together, grow in love together and serve Christ together. Like priority one, this second commitment will take us deeper in Christ and make us more effective in service.

Flowing from priority one and two is our third priority—commitment to the work of Christ in the world. Overflowing in Christ and strengthened by His church, Christians move out into the world for service. When a believer has his or her priorities in order, witness and service are dynamic. Spiritually healthy and vital, Christians are able to dispense the Water of Life faithfully and effectively. Because the primary content of this book focuses on priority three, nothing more will be said here.

At this point, we will discuss several commitments and disciplines relating to priorities one and two. Understanding, embracing and practicing them will strengthen your walk with Christ and your commitment to His church. Upon that foundation, you can consistently serve the Lord with a fruitful evangelistic lifestyle.

Worship

In 1982 I had the opportunity to study with the late David Watson, Anglican pastor and leader in the British renewal movement. He was at Fuller Theological Seminary to teach an intensive course entitled "Renewal in the Local Church." While the primary focus was evangelism, he began by lecturing on worship. What I learned and experienced from Dr. Watson transformed my life. I discovered that worship is filled with power, and that it can usher believers into the presence of God.

In one of his lectures, Watson said that worship:
   • is the first and great commandment: we should "love the Lord [our] God" (Mark 12:30a)

- is the first action we should take when we
come into God's presence—we should "enter his
gates with thanksgiving" (Psalm 100:4)
- is the first response we should make when we
come to Christ: "[Offer] spiritual sacrifices acceptable to God through Jesus Christ" (1 Peter
2:5b)
- is the first mark of the Holy Spirit in our lives:
"God sent the Spirit of his Son into our hearts,
the Spirit who calls out, 'Abba, Father' " (Galatians 4:6)
- was the first sign of the Holy Spirit at Pentecost: "All of them were filled with the Holy
Spirit and began to speak in other tongues"
(Acts 2:4)
- was the first priority of the early church:
"They continued to meet together in the temple
courts . . . praising God" (Acts 2:41–47)
- was their first reaction when in trouble:
"When they heard this, they raised their voices
together in prayer to God" (Acts 4:24a)
- is the first essential when listening to God:
"While they were worshiping the Lord and fast-
ing, the Holy Spirit said . . ." (Acts 13:1ff)
- is the ceaseless language of heaven: "Day and
night they never stop saying: / 'Holy, Holy,
Holy' " (Revelation 4:8b)

Worship must be a regular discipline in a believer's
life. It must be a private as well as a corporate practice. Corporate worship was the focus of my earlier
book, Exalt Him! I refer you there for consideration
of public worship. My focus here will be on private
worship and how it affects our spiritual depth and
maturity.

Robert Webber, in his book *Worship Old and New*, defines worship as a meeting between God and His people.

> In this meeting God becomes present to His people, who respond with praise and thanksgiving. Thus the worshiper is brought into personal contact with the one who gives meaning and purpose to life; from this encounter the worshiper receives strength and courage to live with hope in a fallen world.[27]

Worship involves coming into the presence of God with praise and thanksgiving. We declare the worth of God, praising His character and His mighty deeds. In response, our Father fills and strengthens us for life and service.

Practically, you must incorporate worship into your daily devotional time with the Lord. First, begin by quietly reflecting on the character of God. Scripture reveals Him in majesty so that you can be specific in praise. Consider, for example, that He is:

Sovereign
Omnipotent
Holy
Just
Loving
Merciful
Infinite
Eternal

Likewise, reflect on the names of God revealed in His Word. He is called:

Jahweh-jireh, which means The Lord Provider

Jahweh-rophe, which means The Lord Who Heals

Jahweh-rohi, which means The Lord My Shepherd

Jahweh-shalom, which means The Lord Is Peace

Jahweh-shammah, which means The Lord Is There

In addition, consider what the Father has done in your life, both in meeting daily needs and in providing salvation through Christ. Reflect back to specific times when God answered prayer or intervened in a life crisis.

Now begin to openly praise and worship God. You can do this with your words, your songs and your body. With words, specifically praise and thank God for who He is and what He is doing in your life. Declare His might; give praise for His care and thanks for redemption through Christ. Let your lips present before Him an offering of worship. This is consistent with instructions found in Hebrews, "Therefore, let us continually offer to God a sacrifice of praise—the fruit of lips that confess his name" (13:15).

You can also offer praise to God through singing. Many of the psalms written by David were originally meant for private worship. I find it helpful to keep a chorus and a hymnbook nearby during devotions. I try to select songs that offer praise to Him. Notice, I did not say songs about Him, but to Him. It is important, as an act of worship, to sing praises directly to the Father. Songs such as "Thou Art Worthy," "You Are Lord," "Great Is Thy Faithfulness" and countless others, draw me into the presence of the Almighty.

I also would challenge you to express worship with your body. While that may seem foreign, it was a common practice in Bible times. Various psalms tell us to clap our hands, raise our hands, kneel and even dance before the Lord. Privately, such acts of worship can symbolize surrender, humility, joy and dependance on God. As long as the practice flows from a sincere heart, it is an appropriate way to praise the Lord.

Before ending this discussion on worship, I would like to make two quick observations. First, when praise is part of your devotional time, it affects your entire day. It helps you focus on the Lord. Praise characterizes your attitude and your approach to problem-solving. Thus you are more positive and confident of the Lord's power.

Second, beginning the day with worship affects your work and your ministry. It will encourage you to work diligently as a sacrificial act of worship. In Colossians 3:17 you are told to work at tasks with all your heart, as to the Lord. This means everything should be done to the best of your ability. This brings honor to the Lord and is a sign of your devotion and praise.

Prayer

If you could ask Jesus for one thing, what would that be? Possibly you have a need in your life. Maybe you want to become an effective minister or missionary. You may want to ask for miracle power in order to set the captives free. There might be a burden on your heart that you would have Christ Jesus lift.

Again, if you could ask Jesus for something, what would that be? The disciples came to Christ and asked Him for something. They had seen His miracle power, heard Him preach with authority and felt His tender love. Yet, when they made their request, it did not directly relate to any of these ministries. Instead they said, "Lord, teach us to pray." Of all Christ could give them, their first priority was a life of prayer! By watching Jesus, they learned that prayer was at the heart of His relationship with God and His powerful ministry. They, like Jesus, knew that prayer had to become a vital part of their lives.

Scripture teaches that prayer is an important ingredient for vital Christian life and service. Through prayer, you have communion with God, forgiveness of sin, strength for service, provision for daily needs, power against the enemy and effect upon the lives of others. Prayer links you with your Father in heaven, putting the resources of His kingdom at your disposal. Consider these Scriptures that prioritize prayer:

Pray so that you will not fall. (Matthew 26:41)
Be joyful always; pray continually. (1 Thessalonians 5:16–17a
Is any one of you in trouble . . . pray. (James 5:13)
Devote yourselves to prayer. (1 Corinthians 7:5)
Devote yourselves to prayer. (Colossians 4:2)
Pray for those who persecute you. (Matthew 5:44)
Pray . . . for all the saints. (Ephesians 6:18)
Pray . . . that God may open a door. (Colossians 4:3)

Pray for each other. (James 5:16)

Read Acts and the epistles of Paul, and you can see that prayer was critical in the early church. It was the Christians' supernatural link to power and victory. Likewise, church history gives record of God's men and women committed to prayer. Martin Luther, George Whitefield, John Wesley, George Fox and Charles Spurgeon were mighty men of God. At the heart of their lives was the discipline of prayer. E.M. Bounds, an author who focused on prayer in his writings, said, "The effectual, fervent prayer has been the mightiest weapon of God's mightiest soldiers."[28]

Prayer must be a regular part of your life. It is a discipline that makes a difference! Every day you should communicate with God during your quiet time. And then, throughout the day, you should lift up needs and requests before His throne. Such disciplined practice will draw you closer to God and make you more effective in service.

The obvious question, of course, is, "How should I pray?" Rather than my offering you some novel formula, I will let Christ teach you! After all, the disciples turned to Him with that request, and He taught them to pray. Surely His instructions will guide you also. Jesus said,

This, then, is how you should pray:

"Our Father in heaven,
hallowed be your name,
your kingdom come,
your will be done
    on earth as it is in heaven.

Give us today our daily bread.
Forgive us our debts,
   as we also have forgiven our debtors.
And lead us not into temptation,
   but deliver us from the evil one.''
(Matthew 6:9–13)

What Jesus did was teach a pattern for prayer. You should do more, though, than recite these words. You should use this prayer as a model for your daily life. For example, begin prayer with praise, (''hallowed be your name''). Second, pray about God's will for your life and for the lives of others (''your kingdom come, your will be done''). Third, pray for your needs, believing that God will provide (''Give us today our daily bread''). Then deal with sin in your life. Ask God to reveal areas where you fall short and confess them. Also set free any who have sinned against you (''Forgive us our debts, as we also have forgiven our debtors''). Finally, pray against the enemy who seeks to destroy. Ask the Lord to protect and empower you to overcome his wicked schemes (''And lead us not into temptation, but deliver us from the evil one'').

These five steps of prayer will lead you into effective service and spiritual maturity. It is a pattern that can be easily incorporated into your time of daily devotion. Pray this outline every day, and you will experience the dynamic power of prayer.

Bible study

Christians are people of one book, the Bible. God in His great mercy has chosen to reveal Himself to mankind, and the primary way He does this is through the Bible. If you want to grow in Him and serve His kingdom, you must be devoted to His Word. You must read the Scriptures, study their teachings and pray over their commands. Like food, God's Word is nourishment that gives you health and strength for service. If you want to go deeper with God, you must go deeper into His Word.

The Bible itself says, "All Scripture is God-breathed and is useful for teaching, rebuking, correcting and training in righteousness, so that the man of God may be thoroughly equipped for every good work" (2 Timothy 3:16–17). Notice the three lessons we can learn here about God's Word. First, we see that it is "God-breathed." This means the Scriptures are not just the words of men, but the words of God. While men wrote the text, the Holy Spirit led and inspired them. Second, "God-breathed" means that the Scriptures are living words that have power now. Through the Spirit, the Word of God teaches, rebukes, corrects and trains us. It speaks with authority to our life situation. Third, this passage tells us the goal of God's Word— to equip believers for the Lord's service.

Knowing that Scripture has such power, Paul had this counsel for young Timothy: "Do your best to present yourself to God as one approved, a workman who does not need to be ashamed and who correctly handles the word of truth" (2 Timothy 2:15). This is the challenge you must accept if you hope to go deeper with Christ.

There are two levels of devotion that you should make to His Word. First, you must read the Word as part of your daily quiet time. In order to do this effectively, Scripture reading should be:

Systematic—Do not play Bible roulette, randomly picking Scripture for daily reading. Such practices are seldom helpful and often lead to imbalance. Instead, read Scripture systematically. Either read through the entire Bible, or choose one book at a time. It is easy to set up a schedule that will take you through all of Scripture in a reasonable period of time.

Slow—The key to feeding on the Word does not rest on how fast you read through the Bible. The focus is growth and learning. Take time with the Word, considering what it says and the implications for your life. It is better to read and digest one verse, than to read several chapters and glean nothing from them.

Sensitive—The Scriptures declare that the Holy Spirit is your Guide and Teacher. He is willing to enlighten your understanding of God's Word. You must be sensitive to this ministry of the Spirit, allowing Him to lead. I find it helpful to pray before reading the Bible, asking for the Spirit's help. As I reflect upon a passage, the Spirit often quickens my mind and moves me to act on the Word's instruction.

Sincere—Harvesting the truth of Scripture demands sincerity. You must set aside any preconceived notions, hoping to hear God's voice alone. You should come to Scripture in faith, believing it is the Living Word of God. Like a child without pretense, accept and act upon its truth. It is that simple!

These four guidelines can enrich your devotional time. The Word will daily come alive, even if you read it for only 15–20 minutes. The passages will become food that strengthens and deepens your faith. Such a regular discipline is an indispensable part of personal growth and effective service.

There is a second level of Bible study that I will mention only briefly. You must regularly commit yourself to more intense study of the Word. Whether alone or in small groups, it is a level of inquiry that goes beyond the devotional. Such study involves longer periods of time and resources that reveal the deeper truths of Scripture. Commentaries on Bible books, word study volumes, Bible dictionaries and other tools can help you mine the hidden treasures of His Word. This type of study is necessary and must be an ingredient in your commitment to growth.

Accountability

Reflecting on my Christian walk, I find it is easy to identify several factors that have shaped my faith. Certainly Bible study, prayer and worship are on that list. But just as important has been the matter of accountability. I soon learned that Christians need other believers to lead them on in Christ and to hold them in account on matters of faith. And so, I joined with two other brothers, John Smith and Donn Chapman, and we met regularly for just that purpose. We shared our "souls," read the Word, challenged each other's faith and prayed. We were readily available and committed to each other. This practice affected every area of discipleship, particularly my devotional disciplines.

I have already established the biblical priority of commitment to the body of Christ. Small groups for accountability are one way to practically express that commitment. When well structured, these covenant groups become a place of:

Accountability—Members hold each other accountable for the commitments and disciplines they embrace.

Encouragement—The goal is growth, and the approach is positive and uplifting, focused on edifying each other in Christ.

Openness—The atmosphere should encourage believers to disclose feelings, struggles, hurts and hopes.

Sensitivity—Members affirm each other in Christ, accepting each other where they are, while moving one another on to Christlikeness.

Confidentiality—Whatever is said in the group stays there. This is a necessary commitment that enhances openness.

Prayer—Regular prayer together draws the members before God, the only One who has the power to change people and meet their needs.

Learning—Members seek to discover deeper scriptural truths and apply them to their lives. The goal is not information, but life transformation.

It is important that believers have such small group relationships. If your local church does not coordinate a program of accountability, begin a group yourself. Start by praying that God will lead you to two or three believers who share your interest.

Once you have formed the group, begin to set down basic guidelines and commitments. Decide when and where you will meet and for how long. List the agreed upon commitments regarding attendance, availability, disciplines and foundational covenants. Doing this is important; it becomes the blueprint that guides the group and the glue that holds it together.

Once these foundational understandings are established, decide on your regular format. I have found that the following guidelines keep groups balanced and healthy:

> *Begin with prayer*—This immediately keeps the focus of the group clear. Responsibility should be shared between group members.
>
> *Share from your heart*—Ask each other the question, "How are things with your soul?" This allows for openness and vulnerability. Be sensitive to needs, giving guidance and encouragement from the Word.
>
> *Teaching*—Scripture must come to bear on the group experience. It is best to use either a scriptural theme or a book that walks the group through issues of discipleship. I have found *Called and Committed* by David Watson an excellent resource. Again, share responsibility.
>
> *Prayer*—Follow the teaching time with a season of prayer. Focus on needs in and outside the group. Also, pray that the instruction from God's Word integrates with your lives.
>
> *Fellowship*—It is often best to close with a relaxing time of conversation. Snacks or a meal together can be a good format to bond the group ever closer in Christ.

These simple guidelines can lead your group into a rich experience in Christ. As believers, you can grow closer to Jesus, closer to each other and more effective as servants of the King.

The local church

The New Testament emphasizes the corporate nature of Christ's church. As discussed previously, Christians are to be united, not isolated. One form this unity takes is faithful membership in a local church. This commitment enhances personal growth and makes believers more effective in witness and service.

God's Word gives guidance on how to recognize a healthy church body. It is found in Acts 2:41–47. You will remember that this passage deals with Pentecost and the birth of the church. On that day 3,000 people accepted Christ and became part of the *ecclesia*. Verses 42–47 give us a picture of that New Testament church, which serves as a model for congregations today. Four characteristics can be identified—all of them marks of a healthy local church.

First, a healthy congregation helps believers *grow up*. Notice that the early church emphasized knowledge of God's Word, worship and prayer. It was a place where believers grew in faith and commitment to God. So it should be in all local churches. The Word, worship and prayer must be prioritized, so that believers grow stronger in Christ.

Second, a healthy church causes believers to *grow together*. The picture of the New Testament church is one of people deeply committed to each other. They met in one another's homes, shared meals and helped each other in times of need. There was deep love and commitment. In the Lord's church, people are to be friendly and regular in fellowship and caring. A healthy congregation is a family, deeply committed to one another.

Third, a healthy church causes people to *grow out*. Notice that these early Christians enjoyed the favor of all the people. This means that their witness in the community was positive. Rather than isolating themselves, a healthy body of believers ministers to its community. People care for needs and share the message of Christ with all who will listen. They are known for a positive, powerful presence in the community.

Fourth, a healthy local church *grows more*. The record of Acts is one of growth. The Lord added daily to those being saved. The early believers' witness was a light that consistently brought others to Christ. In just a few years the number of Christians increased to thousands. So today, a healthy church will be a growing church. Where people grow up, grow together and grow out, the body of believers grows more. It is the fruit of good health—a sign of God's blessing.

These four guidelines can be a yardstick, given to us by God, to measure the local church. Obviously, no congregation is perfect. Still, if you want to grow deeper in Christ, you should look for a local church with these characteristics.

By the Power of God's Spirit

I HAD JUST COMPLETED A THREE-HOUR LECTURE on church planting and was making my way back to the office. As much as I love teaching at the seminary, three hours in class is exhausting. I could not wait to close my door, sit down and be still for a while.

As I approached my office, I saw that the door was open and that a student was waiting inside. Admittedly, my first thoughts were self-serving. I wanted to turn and go the other way, seeking out refuge in some secluded nook or cranny. Unfortunately someone might see me, so I chose the next best cop-out— make an appointment with the student for later in the week. That maneuver would allow me to side-step the charge of insensitivity and secretly preserve my need for solitude. With that plan firmly established, I proceeded through the door.

Howard was an upper classman, well-liked and respected on campus. I had him in several classes and was impressed with his devotion to Christ, diligence in service and dedication to evangelism. In my opinion, he was a top candidate for effective pastoral ministry. If only we had more students like him at the seminary.

"Hi, Howard! How are you doing?" My greeting was not that sincere; after all, my intentions were to avoid any real discussion until a more convenient time. Howard, rather than responding to my hollow question with an equally inane remark, broke down crying. In the midst of tears he said, "I'm tired, frustrated and absolutely empty inside. Dr. Wardle, if I do not experience the power of God in my life, I'm going to give up plans for ministry. I just can't keep working in my own strength. Please pray for me!"

At one level I found Howard's remarks a bit surprising—he seemed to have everything going for him. Reared in a Christian home, he had given his life to Christ as a teenager and experienced a clear call to Christian ministry. He had been a leader in his youth group, had gone on to active participation in campus ministries and had taken part in numerous outreach programs at the seminary. From a human perspective, Howard appeared to be on top— effective and a model seminarian.

But on a deeper level, I understood what was happening. Like countless others before him, Howard finally came to realize that " 'Not by might nor by power, but by my Spirit,' says the Lord Almighty" (Zechariah 4:6).

Effective ministry and evangelism is more than having right intentions, right training and right words. You need the Holy Spirit's power working in and through your life. This was exactly what Paul meant when he said, "our gospel came to you not simply with words, but also with power, with the Holy Spirit," (1 Thessalonians 1:5). And, "My message and my preaching were not with wise and persuasive words, but with a demonstration of the Spirit's power,'' (1 Corinthians 2:4).

Experience and training are important, but apart from the power of the Holy Spirit, they are useless tools. Even hard work and diligent service come up empty when done in mere human strength. Howard realized that he desperately needed to ''be filled with the Spirit'' (Ephesians 5:18). It was a pleasure to set aside my selfish agenda and pray with Howard.

David Watson once said:

> From New Testament days to the twentieth century, it remains true that, unless there is a demonstration of the power of the Spirit, the proclamation of the gospel will be in vain. It will not be evangelism.[29]

I have seen people thoroughly trained in friendship evangelism serve faithfully, yet ineffectively. Why? Because they had not experienced the fullness of the Holy Spirit in their lives. Their words were right but absent of spiritual power. Words alone do not set people free from the chains of darkness. It takes *power*.

Evangelism is not a debate or an address; it is warfare. Only those friendship evangelists overflowing with the Holy Spirit can expect to effectively storm the garrisons of Satan. That is why Jesus told His disciples to wait in Jerusalem for the Holy Spirit before beginning their ministries (Acts 1:8). Paul likewise instructs believers to ''be filled with the Spirit'' in Ephesians 5 and in the next chapter speaks of warfare and spiritual armor. Friendship evangelists need to walk in the fullness of the Spirit!

Howard was not the first Christian to cry out in frustration. Since Pentecost, effective ministers, missionaries and evangelists have all reached that same point. Tired of serving in their own power, they have turned to God for His Spirit's infilling. Consider the 19th century evangelist Dwight L. Moody. Few Christians could match the effective ministry of this man. A powerful preacher, he left a mark on society that is still felt a century after his death. Yet he too recognized that it was not by might or power, but by God's Spirit!

Of that day when God visited him with power, Moody said,

> Oh what a day! I cannot describe it; I seldom refer to it; it is almost too sacred an experience to name. . . . I had such an experience of His love that I had to ask Him to stay His hand.[30]

This was not just mental assent to the doctrine of the Holy Spirit. It was an experience of God's power that equipped him for an unbelievable ministry of evangelism and revival! And I believe that what God did for Moody, He will do for every Christian who asks. You can and must experience the Spirit's fullness. It is essential to victorious life and effective service.

In this chapter, I will discuss how to receive the Spirit's infilling and then how to serve in power as a friendship evangelist. I hope by now that you recognize a deep need for this experience. But before addressing God's empowerment in your life, I want to highlight several foundational issues related to the Holy Spirit. My treatment of these matters will be brief, though each point could easily be a chapter in itself. They will be discussed as a basis for a more thorough treatment of the fullness of the Spirit.

The Holy Spirit

What is your image of the Holy Spirit? The *Star Wars* trilogy has likened Him to some impersonal force manipulated by well-meaning warriors who are committed to overcoming the dark side. I remember as a child picturing Him as a ghostly, floating, cloudlike fog that was much more an "it" than a person. It is best to begin by establishing who the Holy Spirit is and what He does for Christians.

First, remember that the Holy Spirit is a Person. The Scriptures teach a great deal about the personal nature of God's Holy Spirit. Isaiah said that He has wisdom, understanding, knowledge and counsel (11:1–2). In John 14 we are told that He comforts, guides and teaches. Paul even pointed out that the Spirit has emotions, warning Christians not to grieve Him. These characteristics are not found in an impersonal, cloudlike force. They belong to the Person of the Holy Spirit.

Second, the Holy Spirit is God. Scripture is clear on this point. Christianity holds emphatically to the belief in one God while recognizing that He manifests Himself in three Persons—all with the same essence, power and glory. Theoretically this tenet is within the mystery of God, and we can never fully grasp it.

The Holy Spirit is one member of this divine Trinity, fully equal and one with the Father and the Son. The Scriptures repeatedly identify the Holy Spirit as God:

Spirit of God (Genesis 1:2)
Spirit of the Lord of Hosts (Zechariah 7:12)
Spirit of Christ (Romans 8:9)
Spirit of the Living God (2 Corinthians 3:3)

His association with the Godhead is also established by:

- the apostolic benediction of Second Corinthians 13:14
- the presence of the Spirit with the Father and Son at the baptism of Jesus
- the command to baptize disciples in the name of the Father, Son and Holy Spirit found in Matthew 28:19
- the divine attributes assigned to Him in Hebrews 9:14, John 16:13, Romans 8:2, Romans 15:30 and Romans 1:4

Who is the Holy Spirit? He is the Person of God, and as such, Christians must accord Him every response Scripture requires of our relationship to the Almighty.

Third, the Holy Spirit is the agent of regeneration. Men and women were meant to walk in a dynamic relationship with God. This is illustrated by the pre-Fall experience of Adam and Eve. They were perfectly in tune with Him, able to worship and enjoy the Father and all of His creation. But, as was stated in an earlier chapter, this blessedness was contingent upon obedience. Adam and Eve were told not to eat of "the tree of knowledge of good and evil" (Genesis 2:17). God warned that disobedience would result in death. As we know, our "parents" did eat of that tree, ushering humankind into death and separation from God.

The death that resulted was more than physical; the greater tragedy was that from then on people were dead spiritually. Their "spirits" were hardened, insensitive to God's leading and unable to live according to His desires. This spiritual death led to constant disobedience, wandering and ultimately the judgment of God.

But, as we know, God did not leave humankind without hope. Centuries before the cross, the prophet Ezekiel spoke of a day when God would renew humankind's dead spirit. He said:

> I will sprinkle clean water on you, and you will be clean; I will cleanse you from all your impurities and from all your idols. I will give you a new heart and put a new spirit in you; I will remove from you your heart of stone and give you a heart of flesh. And I will put my Spirit in you. (36:25–27)

Looking back now, we understand that He was speaking of the new birth available through Christ. When Jesus told Nicodemus that he must be born again, He was speaking of this spiritual experience. Through Christ, men and women can come alive spiritually, walking once again in harmony with God.

This regeneration, available through Jesus, is accomplished by the Holy Spirit. He works this transformation within and then indwells the believer to comfort and guide him or her in life. The "born again" experience is available to all who believe on the Lord. Without spiritual new birth, men and women remain outside of God's eternal family, lost now and forever.

Fourth, the Holy Spirit works within each believer to purify his or her life. Accepting Christ as Savior and Lord does not usher people into perfection. Though born again spiritually, Christians still struggle with sinful attitudes, actions and appetites. That has been my experience and, I am sure, has been yours, and it will be the same for every believer until Christ's return. God has set before us the standard of holiness, but the world, the flesh and the devil war against the very notion. Paul spoke of this struggle in his letter to the Romans: "When I want to do good, evil is right there with me. For in my inner being I delight in God's law; but I see another law at work in the members of my body, waging war" (7:21–23).

But God has not left us alone in this struggle. He has given us His Spirit to "help us in our weakness" (Romans 8:26). The Holy Spirit wants to purify all that is sinful and dead in our lives. If we will surrender to His way, He will help us conquer the sins that enslave us, setting us free to grow stronger in Christ. He also convicts believers of sin, preventing them from stepping beyond God's boundaries of blessing. If we are willing to confess and surrender ourselves to God's will, we can then experience the Spirit's power to overcome sin. In addition, the Spirit helps believers grow in righteousness. Galatians 5:22 lists numerous characteristics of godliness, known as the fruit of the Spirit. The Holy Spirit develops these qualities in believers' lives as they continue to surrender to His purifying work.

God's friendship evangelists *must* say yes to the

Holy Spirit's cleansing. It is essential to life, ministry and witness in the world. Certainly it is neither an easy nor a quick process. But every act of surrender leads to new victory, strength and power for God's children. The Holy Spirit is ready and willing to intercede in the lives of God's men and women, developing them according to His will (Romans 8:27).

Fifth, the Holy Spirit equips Christians with spiritual gifts. The Scriptures teach that believers are given gifts according to the Spirit's will. And the Holy Spirit is the One who determines the particular role each believer will play in the church (1 Corinthians 12:11). God equips Christians to fit in a certain place and perform a certain function in Christ's body.

The pressing question is: How does the Holy Spirit determine the part a Christian plays? The answer, as we discussed in chapter 2, is through spiritual gifts. Remember the definition C. Peter Wagner gave for spiritual gifts?

> It is a special attribute given by the Spirit to every member of the body according to God's grace for use within the context of the body.

According to Scripture, the Holy Spirit gives every Christian one or more of these "special attributes." The majority of spiritual gifts are listed in three chapters of Scripture: Romans 12, Ephesians 4 and First Corinthians 12. These include:

Prophecy	Wisdom
Discernment	Service
Knowledge	Evangelist
Teaching	Faith
Administration	Exhortation

Healing   Pastor
Giving   Miracles
Apostle   Leadership
Tongues   Mercy
Interpretation

Christians are to discover, develop and use their spiritual gifts within local churches. As each Christian does his or her part, united with other members of the body, Christ's work is accomplished.

It is critically important that Christians grow in their understanding of spiritual giftedness. Too many believers are struggling along in ministries for which they were never gifted. Consequently their work lacks both effectiveness and power. God's Holy Spirit has especially equipped every Christian to serve in His body—in a special place and in an effective way. Learning about His gifts will benefit individual believers and the local church body.

Do you know your spiritual gifts? You can. C. Peter Wagner suggests these five steps:

Step #1 *Explore the possibilities*—Learn what the gifts are, what characterizes them, how they function in the body.

Step #2 *Experiment with as many as you can*—Learn which gifts you have and which you do not have.

Step #3 *Examine your feelings*—Because God has put the body together, when you are functioning in the proper area, you will be more effective and feel more fulfilled.

Step #4 *Evaluate your effectiveness*—Gifts are given to produce growth in the body, and the proper exercising of your gift should produce this.

Step #5 *Expect confirmation from the body*—This may be the most important step; other Christians will recognize the gift in operation.[31]

Filled with the Holy Spirit's power!

We now come back to the main focus of this chapter—God's men and women need to be filled with the Holy Spirit. His Spirit wants to indwell, purify and equip us, and every believer must be open to this threefold work. But quite frankly, it is not enough! Christians must go further and receive from God the Holy Spirit's power for Christian service. It is the only way to live and minister in victory.

For three years Jesus discipled 12 men, pouring His life into them and out for them. He taught these men kingdom principles, demonstrated practical ministry and supervised their own efforts of service. It was a combination of theological education and on-the-job training. Jesus did this knowing that He would soon return to heaven and that the work of the kingdom would be in their hands. Several times the Lord told His followers that the Holy Spirit would come to teach, comfort, counsel and lead them. At the time, the disciples were probably unsure what this teaching really meant. But before long they would know and experience Him in a world-changing way.

Graduation day finally came for the disciples. The Teacher was leaving, trusting them to carry on His ministry. They were to preach, teach and heal just as He had done. But on ascension day, moments before Christ returned to glory, He issued one final command. "Wait for the gift my Father promised." Though thoroughly trained in the principles and practices of ministry, they needed one more thing. *Power!* Understanding and ministerial know-how were not enough. The disciples were about to enter a great battle, and only the power of the Holy Spirit could bring ultimate victory. Jesus, anxious to see them reach out around the world, did not want them to go ill-equipped.

We read in Acts 1 and 2 how the disciples obeyed the Lord's command and how they received His promise. For 10 days, 120 followers gathered in a Jerusalem upper room. We are not sure of all they may have said or done, but we are told that they "joined together constantly in prayer" (1:14). Certainly they were also filled with expectation.

On the 10th day, the Holy Spirit came with phenomenal power, filling each follower to overflowing. Afterward, they poured out into the streets of Jerusalem to dramatically and effectively witness for Christ. On that day the church was born with power! The remainder of Acts is an exciting story of evangelism and church growth. In spite of tremendous opposition, Christians spoke with boldness and, at the same time, worked healing, deliverance and signs and wonders by the power of the Holy Spirit. Read Acts and see how the Holy Spirit filled these common people to do ministry in an amazingly powerful way.

The fullness of the Holy Spirit was not reserved only for first century Christians living in the Middle East. He wants to fill believers today just as He did 2,000 years ago. The battle for the hearts of people is just too great for mere human effort.

Secular men and women are trapped in Satan's snares, unable to experience life as God intended.

They suffer from the spiritual and psychological effects of sin. Many have heard the *words* of Christianity but were not impressed. What they hunger for is a genuine demonstration of *supernatural power*. How can I make that statement? Look around. People are moving in ever-increasing numbers to cults and to the occult. As a result they are "rewarded" with greater bondage, deeper scars and utter hopelessness.

Within this context, the friendship evangelist seeks to minister. But obviously, it demands more than good relationships and right words. Freedom from bondage, the healing of deep emotional scars and deliverance from the occult take place only through the dynamic ministry of the Holy Spirit. In today's world God's servants must be Spirit-filled. Then and only then will their evangelistic efforts bear fruit that lasts. Over 100 years ago A.B. Simpson, founder of The Christian and Missionary Alliance, declared:

We must recognize the supernatural ministry of the Spirit, which never was intended to be interrupted, and ought to be expected yet more wonderfully in these last days before the coming of the Lord Jesus Christ. . . . If there ever was an age when the world needed the witness of God's supernatural working, it is this day of unbelief and Satanic power. Therefore, we may expect as the end approaches that the Holy Spirit will work in the healing of sickness, in the casting out of demons, in remarkable answers to prayer, in special and wonderful providences and in such forms as may please His sovereign will—

to prove to an unbelieving world that the power
of Jesus' name is still unchanged and that "all
the promises of God in Him are yea, and in Him,
Amen forever."[32]

Simpson's words were not the lofty, purely theo-
retical insights of an ivory tower scholar. While certainly a respected theologian, A.B. Simpson was an
everyday practitioner. He had personally struggled
early in his ministry due to a lack of spiritual power.
Two Spirit-filled evangelists convinced him to seek
the filling of the Holy Spirit, and that is what he did.
The Holy Spirit transformed Simpson's life, establishing a powerful evangelistic ministry that continues on to this day.[33]

What God has done in others throughout history,
He is willing to do in you. The Holy Spirit wants to
fill your life with power for daily living and service.
You can serve with unusual authority and effectiveness, as the Spirit flows through you as a chosen
vessel. This fullness is more than a mental understanding of the Bible; it is a dynamic and ongoing
personal experience. As God's friendship evangelist,
you can come to the point where you dramatically
sense the Spirit's presence within, guiding and em-
powering your ministry of outreach. Not only is this
the way to world-changing evangelism, it is the path
to a life-transforming encounter with God. Let us
now look at the necessary steps you must take to
receive this gift from on high.

Steps to receiving the fullness of the Holy Spirit

In his letter to the church of Ephesus, Paul wrote,
"be filled with the Spirit" (5:18). This biblical com-

mand is issued to all Christians, compelling them to
seek the Lord's power for service.

*The first step in fulfilling this command is admitting
that you need the Holy Spirit's fullness.* I do not mean
merely understanding cognitively that it is a work
God wants to accomplish in your life. You must inwardly know that your ministry rests on His empowerment, and you must hunger for the experience
with all your heart.

Before embarking in my pastoral ministry, I se-
cured a seminary education. I will be ever grateful
for the countless tools I received there to do the
Father's work. But it took only a few short months in
a local church to learn that knowledge, tools and
methods were not enough. People needed deep inner transformation, and nothing I brought from
seminary would meet that need. I quickly recognized that I needed to be filled with power from on
high. Only the power of God could break through
for these people. If I was to be the agent of that
change, God's Spirit had to first flow in and through
me.

Commitment to friendship evangelism is important. But only the ongoing experience of "fullness"
will insure fruitfulness. My saying this is critical, but
admitting it to yourself and to God is really the first
step. Is God's Spirit right now bearing witness deep
within that He wants to do this work in your life?
Are you willing to prayerfully confess your need to
Him, opening the door to the Spirit's empowerment? If the answer is yes, you are already on the
way to an exciting tomorrow in ministry.

*Taking the time to prayerfully review biblical teaching
on being filled with the Spirit is the second step in*

receiving His fullness. This is important because it will help keep you balanced and firmly rooted in sound doctrine and theology. There are countless opinions and positions on the issue of spiritual power. But for evangelical Christians, all belief and practice must be firmly rooted in God's Word. One helpful way to approach this would be to use a topical Bible, prayerfully surveying the whole counsel of God on the subject of the Holy Spirit. In particular, focus on the New Testament, reviewing the following passages, carefully noting what they teach about the Spirit.

- Matthew 3:11, Mark 1:7–8, Luke 3:16, John 1:3, Acts 1:4–8—these passages all speak prophetically of the Holy Spirit's work in baptizing God's children with power.
- Acts 1 and 2 tell of the dramatic visitation of the Spirit upon the disciples in the upper room.
- Acts 9:1–19 details the conversion of Paul and his subsequent filling with the Holy Spirit.
- Acts 10:1–48 is the story of God's acceptance and filling of the Gentiles through the ministry of Peter.
- Acts 19:1–6 records the account of the Holy Spirit's outpouring on believers in Ephesus.
- Romans 6–8 thoroughly discusses the matter of the Spirit-controlled life.

In addition to these, other Scriptures highlight the Spirit's impact upon believers' lives as they serve the ministry of Christ (Acts 2:4; 4:8; 4:31; 13:9). The Bible clearly teaches that the Holy Spirit will dynamically work through Christians who are ready and willing to be filled to overflowing.

Third, ask the Holy Spirit to identify any hindrances that may be blocking His work within your life. God will not pour out His power upon a vessel that is unprepared or unwilling. Serious self-examination, led by the Spirit, is a necessary prerequisite to empowerment. Common barriers to be eliminated include:

Unconfessed sin. In Ephesians 4:30 Paul warns Christians not to grieve the Holy Spirit. He then lists numerous sins as actions that are unacceptable and that stifle God's work in a believer's life.

Unbelief. Jesus more than once linked belief to blessing. God is free to work in your life only when faith enables you to embrace the unseen and supra-rational.

Fear. In First Thessalonians 5:19, Paul admonishes Christians, "Do not put out the Spirit's fire." People, fearing wildfire, often prefer no fire as a way of maintaining control. Such fear is unwarranted if Scripture is the guide to principle and practice. Trust the Spirit to move you beyond control to dynamic power.

Unbalanced priorities. Jesus Christ must be the ruling principle and passion of your life. His Lordship must be established, drawing you into a deep relationship with Him. If you want to be filled with the Spirit's power, you must keep Jesus Lord of all.

Lack of persistence. Only if you are truly hungry for more will you be able to continue your search for the Spirit's power. Countless believers never break through because they grow weary quickly, giving up before victory comes. Persevere and the Lord will faithfully fill you with power.

The fourth step to receiving the Spirit's power for

service is to turn to God in persistent prayer. Accompanying Jesus' instructions on prayer in Luke 11 is the parable about a man who persistently asks his friend for bread. Even though the friend is asleep, he eventually rises to meet the man's need. Why? Because the man is persistent. He did not give up, but continued to ask. Using this as a model, Jesus then instructs believers to:

> Ask and it will be given to you; seek and you will find; knock and the door will be opened to you. For everyone who asks receives; he who seeks finds; and to him who knocks, the door will be opened. (verses 9–10)

The implication here is obvious. God is not obliged to answer halfhearted prayers, occasionally spoken by fainthearted men and women. But to those hungering for more and determined to lay hold of the blessings of God, the Father promises to give generously. Christ ends His prayer lesson by declaring ''how much more will your Father in heaven give the Holy Spirit to those who ask him!'' (verse 13).

If you want to receive the fullness of the Spirit, pray with persistence. Like Jacob, wrestle until God gives the blessing. As hindrances are removed, the Holy Spirit will be free to come breaking through. But do not grow weary and give up. The Lord *will* be true to His promises, giving abundantly to those who ask, seek and knock. You may find it helpful to join with others in prayer, asking that they intercede on your behalf. This is not only acceptable, it is advisable. And it will strengthen your resolve to see spiritual doors open wide.

It is important to distinguish between faith in God's Word and your feelings. God will be true to His promises. In His time, the Father will set free the Holy Spirit within your life. But the Spirit's infilling may not come when or in the way you anticipated. He touches some people while they are in prayer; He touches others while they are listening to a sermon. He may touch some people when they are alone; to others, He may come while they are in a group. A number of Christians tell of an overpowering experience that made them weak. Many others say that His touch was soft and gentle. The point is: we cannot predict how and when the Spirit will work. It is different for each person. That is why faith in God's promises, not feelings, is the standard believers point to when seeking the Spirit's power for service.

God wants you to minister in power! If you are hungry for His touch and willing to surrender yourself completely to Him, the Holy Spirit has promised to fill you. His Word is your invitation to dynamic empowerment. Respond to Him in sincere prayer, and the evidence of His presence will soon be manifest. The Holy Spirit will penetrate your innermost being, cleansing sin and, at the same time, quickening you to His leading. Before long, new zeal, passion and power will be introduced into your life!

How to minister according to the Holy Spirit

Ron Walborn is a pastor in The Christian and Missionary Alliance. He is an articulate communicator and a solid, biblical preacher. Within the past few years, the Holy Spirit has dramatically filled his life, giving him a new sensitivity to His leading and an extremely effective ministry in evangelism. Ron recently told me this:

> Whenever I go to a person's house, to a sporting event or to other activities, I pray this prayer: "Lord, show me who you have prepared to receive the message of your kingdom in this place." One Saturday while waiting in a lift line at a ski resort in the Poconos, I prayed this prayer. Almost immediately I heard a young man, at least five people behind me in line, cursing and swearing. As I listened to his abusive language, the Spirit of God spoke, instructing me to witness to the teenager.
>
> I quickly told God how impossible this would be since there were four people between us. As I said this, all four people dropped out of line, and the young man and I boarded the chair lift together. Not wanting to argue with the Lord any longer, I began to share about having a relationship with Jesus. As I spoke, tears began to fill the teen's eyes. He said that he had been dating the daughter of a preacher for three months, and that she had been sharing Jesus with him on a regular basis. As we neared the top of the mountain, he said through his tears, "I want to have a relationship with Jesus, too."

The Holy Spirit can lead you in this way, if you will let Him. He can inwardly guide, instructing you to build relationships with specific people, telling you what to say and when. Once the Spirit fills your life, begin to act upon His prompting. Soon you will see that He goes before, preparing the way for people to come to Christ.

In addition, you need to courageously step out in faith to pray for non-Christians. God will often demonstrate His power by meeting needs in their lives. Such "power encounters" verify that the kingdom of God is real and greater than the kingdom of darkness. Take Pat for example, a Spirit-filled Christian woman serving in a New England church. One day she called Dorothy, an unbeliever, to chat on the phone. Dorothy expressed to Pat that she had a very bad sprain and was unable to put any weight on her ankle. Pat wanted to pray for her right then, but did not quite have the courage to do it. Instead, she simply told Dorothy she would be praying for her and hung up.

A short time later, while Pat was praying for Dorothy, she received a phone call. Dorothy was calling to say that the pain in her ankle had just stopped and that she could walk perfectly. This happened on a Thursday and on the following Tuesday, Dorothy went to the home fellowship group Pat attends. During the ministry time, a woman asked for prayer for an inner ear problem that made her dizzy. People gathered around her to pray, and she was instantly healed.

Dorothy witnessed this dramatic work of the Holy Spirit. As a result of her own healing and of the one she had just witnessed, Dorothy accepted the Lord that night.

God is anxious to use Spirit-filled friendship evangelists in just this way. You should pray not only for healing, but for financial needs, marital problems and other life crises. This gives the Holy Spirit the opportunity to manifest His power in the face of darkness. And when non-Christians feel your love, hear the gospel message and witness the power of the Spirit, they will open up to Christ in exciting ways.

Christians of all ages still stand under the command of Jesus—"Wait for the gift my Father promised, . . . in a few days you will be baptized with the Holy Spirit" (Acts 1:4–5).

The Power of Friendship in Evangelism

KEITH BORING WAS IN HIS MID-THIRTIES and had attended church his whole life. It was a routine that began in childhood and continued on into his adult life. Week after week he would take his wife and three children to Sunday school. An hour later he would return and sit with them through the worship service. It was as much a part of his life as work at the bank, the Lions Club and Tuesday night bowling. Attending church was a commitment. But as he would tell you, Keith did not know Jesus Christ as his personal Savior.

Over the years Keith had heard the message of salvation. For the most part, he felt it was religious rhetoric. It had no real impact on his life. If sermons got too personal or emotional, he just mentally "checked out." Any talk about repentance, judgment or the "born again" experience was simply tuned out. His religious life was relegated to 60 minutes a week and no more.

In 1979 his church called a new pastor—me—who was about the same age as Keith. At first, Keith had little involvement with the pastor, but he did notice that people were taking this "religious stuff" seriously. Obviously the pastor seemed to really believe what he was preaching. New people started coming, and the church began to grow. Still, Keith was unimpressed. He could shut this guy off just as he had done with preachers before.

Keith was amazed to discover that I liked to hunt and fish. When we were together on occasion, we would talk about past hunts and the "big one" that got away. Before long a friendship began that led to several outings. We went fishing and hunting together and even began to socialize on a regular basis. Keith would not have predicted it, but he found a deep bond developing between us.

I never pushed the gospel at Keith, making positive reference to Christ only when appropriate. But I did try to live the Christian life before him, and this did not go unnoticed. It was not long before Keith began to reflect on what he was seeing and hearing. And in church, he began to listen more intently to my messages.

Within a year, Keith received Christ as his personal Savior. What did it? Why the difference in attitude? Why did I get through when others had not? It was the power of friendship in evangelism. Our friendship was a bridge, and Jesus walked across that bridge from my heart to Keith's. A few years later Keith gave me a gift—a beautiful sketch of a deer. On the back was the inscription, "Praise God for friendship."

This personal story could be repeated hundreds of times over. Of all evangelistic strategies in use today, none is as effective as friendship evangelism. Countless times I have surveyed classes, asking students,

"What influenced you to receive Christ?" Over-whelmingly the answer comes back, "A friend."

You will remember that according to our working definition, *presence* is a necessary ingredient of evangelism. Christians must establish a caring presence with non-Christians as a foundation for sharing the gospel. They must listen, love and care for unchurched men and women. As we see by the story of Keith Boring, they become friends to these non-Christians, witnessing by word and deed. This consistently opens people to the redeeming message of salvation in Christ.

In this chapter I will lay out seven advantages of friendship evangelism. I pray that they will motivate you to marry two of the most powerful forces on earth: friendship and the gospel of Jesus Christ.

Friendship evangelism is built on love

Have you ever read or seen Thorton Wilder's play, *Our Town*? It is an American classic. Most high school students read this play or perform it as part of their drama education. Wilder's writing vividly portrays the dynamics of small-town life.

In one scene Emily Gibbs dies and is taken to the cemetery. There, she is greeted by many friends and relatives who have already passed away. At one point Emily discovers that she can go back and reexperience parts of her life. The other characters warn her not to do it. They imply that no matter what the memory of life was like, it will not be the same. Still, Emily insists, deciding to return for one of the most cheerful days of her life—her 12th birthday.

The scene changes and Emily finds herself back home. Her mother is coming downstairs to make breakfast on that special day. Emily is excited to see everyone so young and beautiful again. She desperately wants to be noticed, to be heard, to be loved by her family. But Mama and Papa and brother Wally are so busy, so preoccupied. Though they wish Emily a happy birthday, no one really has time to "see" her. After great frustration and hurt, Emily cries out, "Oh Mama, just look at me one minute as though you really saw me. . . . That's all human beings are! Just blind people. . . . I'm ready to go back."[34]

People in our society often feel like Emily did. "No one listens, no one notices, no one loves." We live in a fast-paced, technological age that challenges the notion of personal worth and individual identity. Science says we are little more than apes. The nuclear threat gives scant hope for tomorrow. Abortion sends a message that life is cheap. Technology is depersonalizing the work place. As a result, people feel alone, isolated and often manipulated by those in power over them. The feeling is, "They don't care and I don't matter!"

As a result, people are less vulnerable and more suspicious. They try to hide their true feelings and do not readily trust others—even those reaching out to help. "Surely there is a hidden agenda, an angle, a scam," they suspect. In truth, they are convinced that no one really cares. Walls go up in an effort to keep others out of their personal world.

These attitudes make reaching people with confrontational styles of evangelism next to impossible. Passing out tracts, preaching from street corners, airing church services over radio and television have little effect. People turn the message off, because they are suspicious that evangelists are simply out for "scalps"—or worse, money.

But friendship evangelism is built on a demonstrated love for the individual. You make a commitment to establish a meaningful relationship with an unsaved person. By communicating acceptance and affirmation, doors begin to open for you to proclaim Jesus Christ. As you build relationships of love, those on the receiving end become more receptive to the gospel message. There is a base of trust because the evangelist has been first and foremost a friend who deeply cares, who listens, who notices. Friendship has earned the witness the right to share the gospel.

Friendship evangelism is need-centered

People in our society are hurting—some quite deeply. They may present an appearance of calm, but just beneath the surface is a roiling sea of need. Men and women struggle daily with emotional wounds, relationship problems and the trials of injustice and oppression—wounds that cripple them emotionally, physically and spiritually.

This presents a problem for traditional methods of evangelism. The evangelist often does not get close enough to uncover and address needs. Instead he stands at a distance, failing to link the gospel with specific problems in people's lives. This is tragic, for Christ is the answer to all of life's questions. Evangelistic methods must take Christians beyond formal contact to compassionate, personal concern. And friendship evangelism does this best.

Jack was hired by a Christian college public relations department as a consultant. Administrators wanted to change the image of the institution and appeal to a broader market. Jack had spent 17 years in institutional advancement at several major universities. He had recently formed a consulting firm to help nonprofit organizations with development. He was recommended as a person of integrity, experience and ability.

Jack's initial presentation was first-class. It was obvious that he knew what he was doing and that he could be a great help to the college. Administrators, staff and faculty were impressed with his skill and personality. Jack was upbeat, enthusiastic and easy to be around. He made others feel good and look good. Although no one knew about his spiritual life, the general impression was that Jack was a man who had it all together.

Several members of the faculty developed a meaningful friendship with Jack. They would lunch together and talk about a wide range of subjects. Jack was exposed to the gospel message when he attended devotions at the school. But there was little evidence that it was getting through. His "friends" began to pray for open doors, concerned for Jack's spiritual condition.

On one occasion, when he was alone with one member of the faculty, Jack opened up. He shared how his home situation was in trouble, even disintegrating. It was his second marriage, and domestic conflict from step-children was intense. It was obvious that Jack was deeply concerned and hurting. But no one would have known it unless they got close to him. Only after a base of trust was established could he talk about the inner needs of his life.

The faculty member shared the message of Christ

in the context of Jack's need. The crisis was real, and Jack saw the Lord as the ultimate answer. With barriers removed, he received Christ as the solution to his life's deepest needs. Friendship opened the door, and the Lord entered Jack's life.

Studies show that people in crisis are most receptive to the gospel of Christ.[35] When life's situations are at a certain degree of risk, people begin to search for answers. But they only open up to people they trust. That trust must be built upon genuine relationships as Christians willingly befriend the lost, trusting that over time, doors will open to reveal needs and allow them to proclaim Christ.

Friendship evangelism demonstrates the gospel

People today will not believe the gospel message simply because an evangelist says it is true. Non-Christians want to know, ''Does Christianity really set people free? Does it unburden them from guilt? Does it give power for daily living? Will it give a personal relationship with God?'' That is the rhetoric, but is it the Christian's experience?

People, particularly in the United States, are cynical about Christianity. The climate is not positive, making evangelism difficult at best. Part of the skepticism toward evangelical Christianity is deserved. Certain big-name evangelists and pastors live in ways that run counter to the claims of Christ. Lavish lifestyles, immorality, dishonesty and cravings for power have become national issues. Little wonder that non-Christians question the integrity of the message we believers proclaim.

Years ago poet Edgar Guest put it this way:

I'd rather see a sermon
Than hear one any day.
I'd rather someone walk with me
Than simply point the way.

People do not respond to the message of Christ's
Lordship unless they see it at work in a person's life.
Talking about strength, comfort, forgiveness or direction is not enough. "Is the Christian living what
he or she proclaims? Does the believer really experience the power of Christ?" That is the bottom line
that makes all the difference in a person's attitude
toward the gospel.

Again, this is where friendship evangelism is particularly strong. You build relationships with non-
Christians, spending quality time together. You may
share meals, attend a sporting event, go to a concert
or simply sit and talk. But each setting is an opportunity for your non-Christian friends to observe you
living the Christian life. They want to see your reaction to a crisis, listen to your language, observe your
relationships, analyze your attitudes. All the while,
they look for signs of integrity or hypocrisy. Through
friendship, your non-Christian friends can get close
enough to see the "real you." If you are controlled
by the Holy Spirit, what they see has a dynamic
effect on their lives. They find out that Jesus really
does make a difference!

I am often asked to tell about my conversion to
Jesus Christ. As you would guess, my story begins
with several key people who had a tremendous impact on my life. Their acceptance and love opened
me up to the gospel. Their lifestyles demonstrated
the power of the gospel—a transforming presence

that I soon wanted for myself. They were definitely different, and I wanted what they had. Ever since my conversion I have been convinced that friendship evangelism is a Christian's most powerful vehicle for outreach. With it, believers can both proclaim and demonstrate the power of the Christian life.

Friendship evangelism appeals to most Christians

I quoted some statistics in chapter 3 showing that most Christians are not involved in witnessing and evangelism. One leading Christian evangelist observed that, on average, it takes 1,000 Christians 365 days to lead a single person to Jesus Christ![36] This includes all the efforts of individual Christians, local churches and missionary agencies. This is shocking! It should immediately raise the question, "Why?" What is holding Christian people back from sharing the greatest message ever proclaimed? What keeps them from telling the gospel to everyone they meet?

Certainly to some degree it is ignorance and apathy. Some Christians are not fully aware of the eternal consequences of life separated from God. Others, though it does seem hard to believe, just do not care about the lost. But neither of these factors are true for most believers. Most Christians understand and care deeply. Many believers pray for the lost, give money for missions and invite neighbors to church. But when it comes to actual involvement in witnessing, they choose silence.

As I mentioned in chapter 1, I often begin a class or seminar on witnessing with word associations. I say, "evangelism" and ask students to speak out what first comes to mind. This exercise often reveals two interesting attitudes. First, most Christians feel that witnessing is important. But second, those same believers have a negative feeling about it. Their experiences of evangelism have been less than positive. Words like "insensitivity," "confrontation," "fear" and "anxiety" characterize their image of soul winning. They find confrontational styles of evangelism pushy, impersonal and often judgmental. With this in mind, believers feel they cannot or will not get personally involved. The thought leaves them paralyzed and immobile. This may even be true of you.

But friendship evangelism, by its nature, is not at all like this. Confrontation is replaced with caring. Instead of an insensitive "canned approach," friendship evangelism takes individual life situations quite seriously. Instead of telling the gospel to absolute strangers, you take time to build a meaningful relationship. In that setting, you witness to a friend who has opened the door to the gospel message.

This does not mean that friendship evangelism is as easy as turning on a light. To the contrary, it is costly. You must spend quality time with non-Christians and build relationships over a long period of time. But friendship evangelism is less intimidating and insensitive. And that is what most Christians must address if they are to change their feelings about witnessing. For countless believers, friendship evangelism is the perfect prescription for silence and the best format for sharing their faith. Certainly it has worked for me, and it will work for you, too.

Christians have tremendous friendship evangelism potential

Most, if not all Christians, following their conversion, gradually move away from non-Christian relationships. Within just a few years, fellow-believers become their primary friendship group—the people with whom they share deepest friendships. Where before it was the other men at work, or the bowling team, or the guys at the bar, after conversion it becomes the "brothers" in Christ. Instead of social clubs, service groups and the women at the office, women tend to bond with other Christian "sisters."

At one level this is a natural shift—the Lord calls believers to be a separate people. Many of the activities, conversations and attitudes in these past relationships are unhealthy. New believers need the support of Christ's people and an atmosphere that strengthens their faith. And so, new Christians soon move away from past relationships to new friendships in Christ. Christ so radically transformed their lives that their entire frame of reference changes: "Therefore, if anyone is in Christ, he is a new creation; the old has gone, the new has come!" (2 Corinthians 5:17).

But this tendency creates tremendous problems for evangelism. Christians can disengage so much that they no longer serve as salt and light in society. Believers can be so separate that they lose touch with the world.

I live near the seminary where I teach. For most of the faculty, staff and student body, our entire lives focus on one another. Once, when talking about evangelism to a colleague, he commented, "In truth, I don't really know any non-Christians. I spend all my time with believers." Like so many Christians, radical separation has not been balanced with radical identification, which was, of course, the balance our Lord had in His own life and ministry.

No matter how far you may have distanced yourself from non-Christians, the possibilities in friendship evangelism are still tremendous. Even the most disengaged Christian has at least some involvement with non-Christians. In fact, one author suggests that the average believer has as many as 100 such contacts—people with whom he or she interacts in the day-to-day activities of life. This might include grocery store clerks, people at the bank, parents of children involved in Little League or the local gas station attendant.

Paul Orjala, a specialist in evangelism and church growth, calls this our Evangelism Potential (EP) and illustrates it with the design on the following page.[37]

Properly motivated, believers can readily build meaningful relationships with unbelievers in their EP. Backed by prayer and with minimal instruction, Christians can consistently develop friendships and introduce these new friends to the gospel. This will be the focus of the next two chapters. The potential for fruitful evangelistic ministry is great. It is a challenge and opportunity that I hope you accept. What is your EP?

Friendship evangelism is a lifestyle, not a job

Bob Miller was an active member of his local church. He served on the governing board, taught Sunday school and sang in the choir. Everyone in the congregation knew that Christ was in Bob's heart and that the church was his life. Whenever the doors were open, Bob was there. He was faithful and probably more involved in ministry than anyone else in the fellowship.

EVANGELISM POTENTIAL
IN YOUR
AREAS OF INFLUENCE

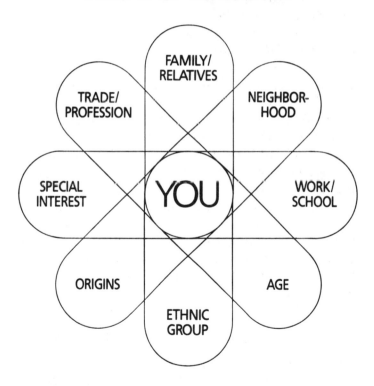

One Sunday the pastor announced a class on friendship evangelism. He appealed to the congregation, asking people to come out and learn to build friendships and share the gospel. Following the service Bob told the minister that he fully supported the idea of evangelism. And while he hoped a great many people would get involved, he could not. Bob was already committed to other ministries and could not add another job to his list. Bob's pastor said he understood, but asked him to at least come to the first class; it would be an introduction to the whole matter of friendship evangelism. Bob did, and what he discovered was exciting: friendship evangelism is not another job, it is a lifestyle. No matter what else you may do, you can always develop friendships for Christ.

Friendship evangelism is not limited to people who have extra time or no other ministry responsibilities in the church—it is for everyone. A person may be a Sunday school teacher, but he or she can still make friends with non-Christians. Board members, trustees, youth workers and elders can consistently reach people for the Lord. A friendship evangelism lifestyle can become a natural expression of a believer's faith in Christ.

Friendship evangelism can be a double-edged sword. On the one side it increases the army of evangelists in any local church. On the other, evangelistically sensitive people are placed throughout the ministries of the body. Sunday school teachers, choir members, ushers, nursery workers and group leaders share a basic commitment to evangelism. People working at different jobs all share a concern and compassion for the lost. While still active in areas of service other than evangelism, they can sensitively point people to Christ.

You may be much like Bob, actively involved in your local church. As you consider evangelism, you may wonder how to fit it into your schedule. Remember, it is a lifestyle, not another job at church. It involves sensitively caring about others, developing friendships and sharing the message of Jesus. I believe any committed Christian would say yes to that. Would you?

Friendship evangelism can span the follow-up gap

Brenda Jefferson was standing by the kitchen sink washing the dinner dishes. Her three-year-old twin boys were outside the apartment building riding their "big wheels." Dana, her six-year-old daughter, was at the dining room table coloring. Suddenly there was a knock at the door. Brenda knew it could not be her husband, for he was working until midnight. Maybe it was a neighbor from across the hall.

Brenda was startled when she opened the door and found three strangers standing there. Their smiles and pleasant manner quickly put her at ease. After a quick introduction, the three visitors said they were from a neighboring church. Brenda was hesitant when they asked if they could come in and talk with her, but she finally welcomed them into her living room.

Over the next 45 minutes, the two men and one woman clearly shared the gospel of Jesus Christ. They were sensitive, caring and patient with Brenda, reviewing anything she did not understand. Brenda unexpectedly opened up, talking emotionally about personal discouragement and fear. The visitors pointed Brenda to Christ's love and His willingness to walk with her through life's trials. Before the hour passed, this young mother made a decision for Christ. She prayed to receive His love and forgiveness, committing all of her tomorrows to Jesus.

The three "evangelists" were overjoyed and assured Brenda that Jesus was true to His Word. They encouraged her to read the Bible, pray and be sure to attend church the next Sunday. It was obvious that Brenda was deeply touched and sincere. She had made a decision for Christ.

That was the last time Brenda ever saw the three visitors. She wanted to go to church, but received no support for the idea from her husband. Even when she thought of going, the question was "Where?" Brenda did not know anyone in the neighboring churches. For several weeks she thought about church, but never went. Before long, she did not think about it at all, and the new "feeling" she had for Christ grew dim. Brenda had made a decision, but unfortunately never became His disciple.

As you know, the goal of evangelism is not registering decisions, but making disciples. This, and this alone, is the imperative within the Great Commission. Evangelism that aims at anything less falls short of the mark. Yet, far too often there is a large gap between people who make decisions for Christ and those who become disciples. The story of Brenda can be illustrated by hundreds of examples with the same result. Many people who respond to the message of salvation never move on to discipleship.

Why does this happen? This problem has been called "the follow-up gap." As the phrase implies, the reason for the difference between those receiving Christ and those becoming His disciples is follow-up. Follow-up refers to the care and instruction given to a new convert once he or she turns to Jesus. When personal attention and follow-up are given, people most often move on to discipleship. When follow-up does not occur, the new convert seldom moves on to maturity in Christ. Studies have shown that the more impersonal the evangelistic method and follow-up, the higher likelihood of short-term commitment.[38] And in reverse, the more personal the care after conversion, the greater chance of lifelong discipleship.

Once again, this is where friendship evangelism is particularly strong. When a person turns to Christ through friendship evangelism, he or she is not a nameless face in the crowd. The convert is a personal friend, uniquely loved and accepted by the Christian witness. Time, conversation and commitment have preceded any turning toward the Lord. The new convert is a friend, and it is highly unlikely that follow-up will not occur. The natural bridge of friendship serves as a link to ongoing care and instruction. As a friendship evangelist, by any one of several methods, you can lead your friend toward responsible Christian discipleship. The bond of love motivates you to encourage the new convert through the doorway of faith. With friendship evangelism, the follow-up gap is eliminated. Decisions lead to faithful disciples.

Friendship evangelism is powerful! These seven advantages are but an introduction to this exciting method of reaching the lost. I hope they will motivate you to faithfully make friends for Jesus Christ. Considering the potential, friendship evangelism deserves your most sincere attention and serious investment. It is an effective way to live an evangelistic lifestyle and consistently influence others with the gospel. That, my friend, is our greatest privilege and our awesome responsibility. From here, let us go on to identify concrete steps for building relationships and sharing the message of Christ.

CHAPTER
7

How to Be a Friend

FRIENDSHIP DOES NOT JUST HAPPEN! It takes time and commitment to develop a genuine relationship. Because of this, true friendships are rare; most people are not willing to pay the price. It takes determination to eliminate the obstacles that often keep people apart. Barriers to true friendship include:

Self-centeredness—We have a tendency to be more concerned with our own needs and desires than those of others.

Busyness—We are so preoccupied that we have little time to listen, notice and care.

Jealousy—We harbor a resentful, competitive spirit that makes people rivals rather than friends.

Faultfinding—We focus on the traits in others that we do not appreciate, rather than accepting people as they are.

Manipulativeness—We build a relationship for our own benefit, to take rather than to give.

Privacy—We are unwilling to be open, honest and real; facades, pretense and a reluctance to share keep our friendships shallow.

Gossip—We betray another's confidence by sharing in public what was whispered in private.

Unavailability—We will not give friendships the time they require. Absence does not make the heart grow fonder; it simply causes people to drift apart.

Only if you are willing to work through these problems can you hope to develop friendships that count. Like most things in life, anything worthwhile takes hard work. Yet in the end, genuine friendship is its own reward. And it can lead to open doors and tender hearts toward Christ.

You are, no doubt, familiar with the saying: "If you want a friend, you have got to be a friend." While most generalizations tend to be weak, this one is right on. If you want to bond with another person, you must accept the responsibility of being a friend. You must take concrete steps, moving from a casual acquaintance to a meaningful relationship—steps that will take you beyond barriers to building a trusted friendship. That is the focus of this chapter. We will discuss the commitments you must make in establishing trusted relationships with non-Christians. As I have already suggested, it is a costly though rewarding process. Are you willing to pay the price?

Pray for open doors

As you consider establishing friendships with non-Christians, start with prayer. It is your invaluable ally in all you do as a Christian. Prayer puts you in touch with the living power of God, which is essential to your work as an evangelist. Paul, in Colossians 4:3, asked believers to pray for open doors. He recognized that Satan wants to restrict the spread of the

Lord's gospel. It is the enemy's desire that all perish, that all suffer eternal judgment, that none hears God's message of salvation in a life-changing way. It is not enough that you intend to break that bondage. In all aspects of evangelism you must be empowered by the Holy Spirit, and prayer is the key to that empowerment.

Evan and Donn were friends, both attending the same college in western Pennsylvania. They came from Christian homes and were committed to the Lordship of Christ. Like most college students, they had the normal struggles with rebellion, yet they shared an honest desire to live for Jesus. Church services and Christian fellowship groups were a regular part of their lives.

On that same campus was a young man who did not share Evan and Donn's faith. His lifestyle was for the most part inconsistent with the gospel and his appetites ungodly. Church was little more than ritual, and most Christians turned him off. Their lives seemed boring and unattractive. When he was asked to go to the campus Christian activities, he always had more than enough reasons to say no. Under most circumstances he shared little in common with the Christians and seldom socialized with them.

It turned out that Evan and Donn had something in common with this fellow. All three were involved in varsity sports, so they would regularly spend time together. Though their lifestyles were not compatible at all points, there was the potential for a meaningful friendship. Recognizing this, Evan and Donn not only began to spend time with this non-Christian, they prayed for him. Their prayers had two specific focal points: they wanted the Lord to bless their friendship and they wanted Him to open doors so they could present the gospel to their friend.

Over the next two years a deep bond developed between these three. They spent much time together and grew to genuinely love one another. During this time Evan and Donn continued to pray. On occasion, they shared the gospel of Christ. Although they saw no immediate response, the message was getting through. Finally one evening, this young man responded to the gospel Evan and Donn had presented. Prayer laid the foundation and friendship opened the way. I know this story well—I was that young man!

Friendship evangelism begins with prayer. It is the first step in establishing relationships with those outside of Christ. Begin by asking the Lord to lay a particular person on your heart. Who in your EP— your evangelism potential acquaintances—would Jesus have you befriend? Pray, and the Lord will lead you to the person of His choosing. Also, pray that doors will open for you to get acquainted. Believe me, the Holy Spirit can initiate opportunities you never dreamed possible. Pray, too, for the Spirit to begin working in your potential friend's heart. He will faithfully break down barriers and prepare that one to receive the gospel of Christ.

It is equally helpful to enlist fellow Christians in prayer. When you bind yourself together with other believers in prayer, things happen. Christian unity is a mighty weapon against the strongholds of Satan. I always encourage friendship evangelists to find two prayer partners. Ask these coworkers to faithfully petition the Lord on your behalf. Have them join you in prayer, asking God to find the right person, open doors to friendship, sensitize hearts and empower you to proclaim the gospel. Once you see the dynamic power of prayer, it will become your first priority in outreach.

Be interested and concerned

True friendships develop when people see that you are both interested and concerned about them. This is an essential principle of friendship and critical to establishing relationships with non-Christians. As we already discussed, busyness and self-centeredness are giant walls that restrict potential friendships. Like at Jericho, these barriers must crumble before there can be victory. People need to sense that you are genuinely interested in them. This is not what most people in today's world experience from others. Men and women are too busy, only interested in "their own worlds." People seldom stop, listen or care about anything or anyone. If you take the opposite approach, you may unlock doors that have been closed for years.

Lois Volstad is a coworker at Alliance Theological Seminary. For several years she has been my secretary, helping particularly with the Center for Evangelism. Students have warm, affectionate feelings toward Lois. To many, she is the "friend of the students." Exactly how did she get this reputation? She earned it through love and concern.

At least once a day, I see Lois talking with some student. Or, to be more accurate, she is sitting there listening. Students talk to Lois about their classes, financial burdens, relationship problems and matters of spiritual growth. They share almost everything imaginable with her. Why? Because first of all, Lois is always interested in the students and their concerns. She never comes across as being too busy. If something is important to them, it is important to Lois. Students know that and readily open up to her.

Second, students find Lois a friend because she actively cares. While listening she empathizes, and she often promises to both pray and do what she can to help. And, as they know, Lois has proven to do just that—more than once I have had to listen as she petitioned me on their behalf! Without concern for herself, Lois will put her loyalty and friendship on the line when necessary. All this interest and caring has reaped a priceless harvest of friendship for Lois.

If you are going to build friendships, interest and concern are indispensable ingredients. Nothing can be too silly for your interest or too petty for your concern. If people sense otherwise, they will keep walls high and doors locked and bolted. What is important to them must be important to you. You must be willing to listen as people talk about their health, family or hobbies. You need to show concern for their problems, decisions and needs. This takes work for most believers accustomed to ignoring or not caring about the world of non-Christians. But it is the only way to establish true friendships.

Just today Lois sent me a note with a quote that really says it all: "People want to know how much you care, before they care how much you know." She is right! And if we hope to make friends for Christ, interest and concern are indispensable. Ask the Lord to open your eyes and heart to the people around you. Soon, you will see the joys and burdens of others. Once they see that you are interested and that you genuinely care, they will trust you enough to listen to what is on your heart also. Then and only then will you be able to tell them about Jesus.

Build on common interests

Linda Kolano was an active member of the first church I pastored. The Lord had touched her deeply, and in response she gave all she had to Him. Linda faithfully attended worship and Bible study, served on the administrative board and supported our ministry. My wife, Cheryl, and Linda became fast friends. They found a common bond in Christ and had numerous shared interests. As a result, their friendship grew deep and genuine.

While Linda and her son Jason came to our church, her husband Joe did not. He did not oppose Linda's commitment to the church, but he was not particularly interested himself. When I first met Joe, he was talkative and pleasant. But he showed no evidence that surrendering to Christ was even an option. Joe was satisfied with life as it was and saw no need to change.

More than once Linda voiced deep concern about her husband's salvation. She prayed for him faithfully and shared Christ whenever appropriate. Cheryl and I joined in praying for Joe. Since I was already committed to friendship evangelism, my prayer was that doors would open for a relationship. I was amazed at how fast the Lord answered that prayer.

Clarence, another man in the church, owned a cottage in the mountains. Several times he recommended that I go there for rest and fishing. Trout streams were numerous and, at the right time of

year, full of fish. One April I was especially drained
and decided to accept his offer. I set aside three days
for solitude, rest and relaxation by the stream. But
as I began making plans, the Lord put Joe on my
mind. I suddenly remembered that he liked to fish.
Could this be the open door about which I had been
praying?

With little time to prepare, I asked Joe to go with
me to the mountains. In some ways it was a bold
step; we really had not spent any meaningful time
together. Three days in the mountains could be a
real trial-by-fire for any relationship. But I felt the
Lord's leading and by faith extended the invitation
to Joe. After checking things out at work, he agreed
to go along. Fishing was to become our common
ground.

The trip took four hours, and as we drove we
got acquainted. In the context of sharing my background, I had opportunity to proclaim the gospel of
Christ. But for the most part we just talked. Over
the next three days we cooked together, fished together and shared in lengthy conversations. More
and more the subject of Christ came up. And more
and more we began to bond as friends. By the time
we were ready to start back home, two important
things had taken place: we had become friends, and
Joe had given his life to Jesus. Three days earlier we
were nearly strangers; now we were brothers in
Christ!

You can effectively initiate friendships by building
upon common interests. Find out what hobbies people have, what they enjoy reading or where they like
to dine. Use these interests as a place to start your
relationship. I have established friendships around

sports, Little League, social causes and woodworking. Each common interest opens the door to go deeper. The more time you spend doing things together, the more genuine the friendship becomes. Soon, opportunities to share Christ will come. If you honestly do not have any common interests, learn to appreciate the interests of the other person. Let him or her open your world to new experiences. It will only serve to strengthen the potential bond you want to have with this person.

Obviously, building on common interests takes time. You must open up your schedule and your plans. It is the price you must willingly pay to be effective in friendship evangelism. If you think the cost is too high, think about Jesus. He left glory to identify with our world. Should you not be equally willing to walk with non-Christians, identifying with them as Christ did with you? It is the way of genuine friendship and the priority of fruitful evangelism.

Give, demanding nothing in return

Ted W. Engstrom, former president of World Vision, has written an excellent book entitled, *The Fine Art of Friendship*. In it he tells the following story that illustrates giving and demanding nothing in return. I never cease to be challenged by this powerful account.

About one month after his parents learned their son, "P.J." Dragan had leukemia, the child began receiving a variety of get well messages. He received gifts, cleverly written letters, poems, and drawings. The presents all came from an unnamed party called "Magic Dragon." The special trademark of Magic Dragon's gifts was a big green bow.

As the weeks and months wore on, little P.J.'s treatments grew long and painful. But there was one consolation. Magic Dragon's surprises arrived at the house with clockwork regularity. P.J.'s favorite gift was a stuffed dragon—a friend that became more realistic to the boy as the disease progressed.

P.J.'s father was a Detroit policeman. At one point, he tried to track down Magic Dragon's hidden identity. However, he changed his mind when he discovered the trouble to which Magic Dragon had gone in order to cover his or her tracks.

When little P.J. went into the hospital, the prized toy dragon received the same treatment the boy did. When a bandage was put on P.J., the dragon got one too. That little stuffed toy with the green bow pulled P.J. through some of the most difficult times of his illness.

Unfortunately, five-year-old P.J. lost his battle, and shortly after listening to his favorite record, "Puff the Magic Dragon," the brave little boy died. Hundreds of friends and relatives paid their final respects to P.J. and contributed to the vast array of flowers that occupied most of the room where his little body lay. As you would have expected, in the middle of the display was a gigantic bouquet of daisies tied affectionately together with a big green bow.

"Magic Dragon," if you're reading this book, I want to say thank you from all of us whose lives are a lot different because of what you did.

You made no demands on P.J., and you chose anonymity to do what you were moved to do.[39]

Too many people are in relationships for what they can take, not for what they can give. Their affection is often conditional and manipulative. "I care about you, because you can give me something." It may be fame, finances or just good feelings. But for countless people, friendship is only a means to an end.

Christians should build friendships based on giving, not on receiving. They must get close enough to identify needs and do their part to help. Love should go to the unlovely, support to the weak, security to the fearful, food to the hungry and, most of all, Christ to the lost. Christians cannot only associate with the popular or powerful. As instructed in the book of James, Christians should not show favoritism in hopes of some reward. They cannot keep score on how many times they have helped someone, planning to cash in at a later date.

While counseling a couple considering divorce, I listened as the husband said these words, "I'm just not getting anything out of this relationship." His wife then echoed the same evaluation. Sadly, they were totally missing the point. Relationships are best founded on giving, not on receiving. Then and only then are our motives right. True love is totally "other person" centered, as opposed to self-centered love. Step out and give, demanding nothing in return. Most likely, you will reap a harvest of love. But that cannot be your motivation. Just learn to give, and let the Lord take it from there. Only then will you truly "be a friend."

Be available

Can you imagine what it was like for the disciples of Jesus? They had open and constant access to the Lord. For three years they walked and talked with Him. Jesus taught them kingdom principles, supervised their ministries and prepared them for the future. They traveled at His side, ate with Him and shared in the Lord's glorious miracles. What a tremendous privilege! Jesus was willing to spend quality time with His disciples. He was there when they needed Him, always available. His friendship was deep and genuine, holding nothing back from those He loved.

We too experience the availability of the Lord. One promise of the Scriptures says, "Never will I leave you; / Never will I forsake you" (Hebrews 13:5). Jesus says, "And surely I am with you always, to the very end of the age" (Matthew 28:20b). Through the presence of the Holy Spirit, the Lord is always with us. He is present for fellowship, direction, instruction, strength and help. If we have a need, we know Christ is there. If we are facing trial, the Lord will stand with us. When suffering from persecution or rejection, Jesus will be our strength. One clear commitment of the Lord's friendship is constant availability. I personally find great comfort in the Lord's nearness and dependability.

Do you make yourself accessible to others? Would friends say that you are available, dependable and near in times of trouble? Are you modeling your friendship after the example of our Lord? These are important questions, and your answers speak volumes about your understanding of true friendship.

Availability is foundational to meaningful relationships. If you hope to grow close to the non-Christians God has laid on your heart, be there for them!

Peter Burgo is my friend. I do not mean we know each other informally. He is truly my friend—dependable, accessible and always there when I need him. We met just over four years ago in Johnstown, Pennsylvania. He was, at the time, a non-Christian. Peter came to me for some help in a tough situation. I knew Christ was the answer and prayed that a friendship would develop between us. Soon we were occasionally skiing, fishing and socializing together. Within a short period of time the Lord came into Pete's life. And our friendship bonded all the deeper.

Since that time, Peter and I have become true brothers in Christ. I could not calculate the many hours we have spent together. We have laughed, cried, prayed, praised, rested and worked side by side. And every occasion has been a blessing, a special gift from above. There are many characteristics of Peter's friendship that I cherish. But most of all, I am thankful that he is always available. No matter what the need or circumstance, I can count on Peter.

I could illustrate Peter's commitment to availability with dozens of examples. I wish I had the space here to do so, as a tribute to his friendship. But this one story will say it all. I must travel frequently as part of my responsibilities at the seminary. On one occasion I was making a trip to San Francisco and needed a ride to the airport. Pete immediately volunteered. At the airport we learned that the flight would be delayed six hours. Instead of waiting there, Pete suggested that we go back home so I could spend the time with my family. The trip was going to be over two weeks long, and I was glad to squeeze in all the extra time at home I could. So we made the 35 minute drive back home.

Six hours later Pete dropped me off at the airport again. I waited for an hour, only to find that the flight was cancelled. It was by then 11:00 p.m., and I could not get a flight out until the next morning. I called home, asking my wife to make arrangements for me to be picked up. Again Pete was there! Not once did he even hint that it was an imposition. He was a true servant through the entire ordeal.

The two weeks away were not easy ones. My schedule was demanding, and I ended up getting sick. Several times Pete called, encouraging me with prayer and support. He did not have to do that, but I am surely glad he did. When I arrived back in New York, it was Pete who greeted me. Exhausted, I just drew from his well, comforted by the genuine love of a true, dependable friend. No one will ever know how much he ministered to me as we drove back to Nyack.

If you hope to be a friend, be available. Allow people to call on you in times of need. Let them see that you are accessible and anxious to be there for them. Such Christlike commitment to others will endear them to you. They will trust you, open up to you and lean on you in tough times. And a foundation will be laid for a lifelong friendship. Even the toughest non-Christian will soften to the glorious message of Christ.

Learn to listen

In 1987 Dr. Reginald Johnson, from Asbury Theological Seminary, was invited to speak at our faculty retreat. For two days he challenged us on matters of spiritual development. Dr. Johnson particularly reminded us that as teachers, we must lead students toward spiritual maturity. He gave us keen insights and practical suggestions that put most of us back on track. At one point he made the following observation: "It is better to be unavailable than inattentive." Wow! That statement flattened me. I have never forgotten those words nor their power to rebuke me at a point of true weakness.

More than once close friends have mentioned that I have a problem listening. My mind, filled with ideas and focused on other tasks, does not easily shift its attention. Sometimes people will talk to me, stop in mid-sentence and say, "Are you listening to me?" I cannot lie, because my body language has already given me away. Restlessness, shifting positions, glancing at my watch, are all telling the speaker that I am not giving them my attention. Thankfully, most people have been patient with me about the whole matter. But unfortunately, it has at times deeply hurt people who wanted more than my presence—they needed my attention.

Recognizing my problem enabled me to change. Though it has not been easy, I am making progress as a listener. Through friends and study, I am learning key principles of listening. I would like to share them with you, hoping that they will help you be both available and attentive.

To begin with there are two important benefits of listening. First, it will help you build meaningful friendships with others. As already discussed, ours is a fast-paced world. Busyness is the order of the day and, for many, the standard of productivity.

The agenda for busyness is for the most part self-centered. People tend to "do their own thing" with little time for others. Countless people, as a result, feel invisible and unimportant.

When you take time to listen, you send a powerful message. You are saying to the other person, "I care. You are important. Your concerns are worthy of my attention. I want to know about your world." Listening becomes a magnet that draws two people closer and closer together.

Second, listening opens doors for communicating the gospel. That sounds almost contradictory, yet it is true. Instead of rushing in to talk, be quick to listen. As you do, not only will you better understand the other person's world, you will earn the right to speak. By listening, you will be heard all the better. People closed to the gospel will open up to hear its message, once they hear your silent message of concern. Listening is the way to make friends and open doors for the gospel.

As I have suggested, listening does not come naturally. Most people need help, as I did, to become truly attentive to others. I have found the following guidelines helpful in sharpening listening skills. Prayerfully consider them as you attempt to truly "hear" others.

> *Evaluate your listening habits.* Would people find you a good or a poor listener? Ask some friends. Their feelings are your best test.
> *Practice listening by being silent.* I once was reminded that the word listen and silent have exactly the same letters. They go together! Silence

helps you discriminate between sounds, so you know what you are hearing.

Learn to look for people who need a listening ear. Most people who need to talk will come to you. But many others who are upset or hurting send only signals. Withdrawal, aggressive behavior and unusual quietness may mean they need to talk.

Consider how you feel when someone has not heard you. Put yourself in another's shoes. What would it be like to desperately need someone to listen, only to find them inattentive? I doubt we would appreciate such insensitivity.

Find a time and a place to really listen. Distractions must be eliminated. Find a quiet place, at a time that is best, where you can hear concerns clearly—louder than anything else.

Identify negative actions that say "I'm not listening" and eliminate them. Glancing away, looking at a watch or clock, continuing to write, shifting positions, all say "I don't care." Work hard at eliminating these signals from your silent vocabulary.

Know when and how to respond. Do not be quick to give advice or respond with cliches. Most of all, people want you to listen and communicate concern. Focus on that response more than any other.

Right now, all around you are broken, lost men and women. They feel lonely, abandoned and unimportant. Every day they hurt, yet they find few people who care. Their voices may be silent, but they cry out for someone to listen. Are you able to hear their desperate plea?

Invite others into your world

I have not had the pleasure of personally meeting Dr. Brian and Sharon Wilson. But their niece, one of my students, has shared this story with me. In turn, I want to tell you about this wonderful couple, committed to opening their world to others.

For 10 years, Brian and Sharon served as medical missionaries in Zaire. But for the last 13 years, the Wilsons and their four sons have lived in Raleigh, North Carolina. Brian is an orthopedic surgeon in a local hospital. While they no longer serve as foreign missionaries, they still minister Jesus Christ to the lost and broken. Over the years Brian and Sharon have invited literally dozens of people into their world—people struggling with loneliness, rejection, abuse, addiction and despair. The Wilsons have opened their home as a place of healing and support. Some people stay a few days. Others live with them for months, receiving love, understanding and direction. And many leave with the greatest gift of all, Jesus Christ.

For example, two years ago the Wilson's pastor told them about a woman who had fled from her abusive husband. Deeply touched by the situation, they made contact with her and invited the woman to stay with them as long as necessary. For two and a half months she lived in their home. They gave her love, acceptance and protection from her husband, who threatened to kill her. During that time the young woman came into a dynamic relationship with the Lord.

The Wilsons did not just minister to the woman; they prayerfully made contact with her husband.

The Lord opened the right doors, and before long they convinced him to get counseling. A friendship developed, and he too came to know and experience the saving power of Christ. Today this couple is reunited and centered in Jesus. The husband is now the Wilsons' family dentist, and the two families are close friends. Their story is one of many in the Wilsons' experience. They are a living testimony to the transforming power of friendship.

The example of Brian and Sharon may be beyond your present abilities or experience. But having broken people live with you is not the only option to openness. You can invite people into your world by having them over for dinner. Sharing a meal in a person's home is a meaningful symbol of friendship. You are inviting them into a treasured part of your world. A home is personal and private. Asking someone to enter that space shows that you value their relationship with you. Likewise, ask people to take part in other important events and relationships in your life. Include them in special times with friends, like a picnic or barbecue. Ask them to go with you to church-related events, where they can meet your Christian friends. It may be a potluck supper, family retreat or special services of some kind. By doing this, you bring people into the valued commitments of your life. Friends know this and will respond with deeper love and loyalty.

As with all principles of true friendship, openness does not come easily. You must be willing to surrender any selfishness, truly sharing precious time, places and relationships with others. But that is the true nature of Christian service, the example of our Lord. In return, you will have the opportunity to touch people more deeply than you ever thought possible. And through friendship, you can share the great message of life in Jesus Christ!

Conclusion

As you can see, true friendships do not just happen. Committing yourself to building relationships with non-Christians is costly. It probably will mean changing old habits and opening up to a whole new way of relating to others. Friendships take prayer, time and active caring. You must learn to listen, love and be ever dependable and available. Instead of shutting people out, you must willingly open your world to others. These principles are the nonnegotiable ingredients of true friendship. In return, people will respond to your love by listening to the message of life you so desperately want to share. Friendship is an investment you cannot afford not to make—for yourself, for others and for Christ.

How to Share the Gospel

CHERYL AND I WERE DELIGHTED when Cara came home announcing, "I have been asked to be in the Christmas pageant." Our daughter was beaming with excitement as she told us about her special part. Cara read over her lines and showed us the words and music of a short solo. She was thrilled. Cheryl and I had to fight an overwhelming sense of pride. With great anticipation, we were about to experience yet another rite of passage as parents. Our beautiful daughter was to be an angel in the annual junior Sunday school play!

Cara quickly learned that her privileged "position" carried with it responsibility. She had to memorize lines, practice her solo and regularly go to rehearsal. Preparation was not fun, and she needed Mom and Dad's constant encouragement. We reminded her that people would be attending the play and watching her every move. That helped motivate Cara to keep memorizing and practicing.

The day for the Christmas pageant finally came. We all joined Cara in preprogram jitters. Cheryl helped her dress, while our son Aaron teased her with promises of raw eggs. I prayed! Questions danced in my mind. "Will she be too nervous to speak? Does she know her lines? Will she sing loudly enough for everyone to hear? Is she enjoying this more than I am?" I surely hoped so!

Cheryl, Aaron and I waited anxiously for the play to begin. Lights suddenly went dim, enabling us to faintly see children finding their places on stage. Proud parents and relatives strained to catch a glimpse of the play's star (their own child of course!). Within minutes the pageant began, the precious children telling the story of Christ's birth.

Cara was not yet on stage, adding to our excitement and anxiety. Suddenly, our angel appeared, nervously but on cue. Her lines were delivered, almost with ease, and her solo was beautiful. Though I could not tell anyone else, she was definitely the best! We were all delighted and relieved as Cara disappeared from stage to await "the reviews." She had prepared well. When the time came, Cara knew what to say and when to say it, and she did it the best she could. We were thankful and admittedly more than a little proud.

I would like to ask you an important question. When the time comes, will you be prepared to share the gospel of Christ? You have been chosen for a special role—Christ's messenger. Unlike a child's play, lives will be hanging in the balance. But much like Cara's experience, the time for you to speak will come sooner than you think. Will you be prepared? Will you recognize the opportunity and know what to say and when to say it? Will you be sensitive to the Spirit's leading and be able to actually introduce your friend to Christ? If you are building relationships with non-Christians, the door will eventually open for you to share the gospel. You must know how to guide a person, step-by-step, to a personal relationship with Christ. That will be the focus of this chapter.

Identify opportunities and open doors

It is important for you to develop "evangelistic eyes." By that I mean the ability to recognize, through verbal and nonverbal signals, opportunities to share the gospel of Jesus Christ. I often hear Christians remark that they seldom have a chance to witness. The opportunities were probably there, but unfortunately, they never recognized the potential. They were not conditioned to see what was before them.

I was once walking in the woods with my dad. He suddenly stopped and said, "Look at that." I stared in the direction he was pointing but saw nothing at all unusual or exciting. My father said, "There's a rabbit sitting there in the briars." I stared all the harder and still saw nothing. Finally, I practically put my face in the rabbit's nose, and it went bouncing away. Then, of course, I saw it! My dad's eyes were sharper than mine. He quickly identified what I could not see.

Likewise, as a friendship evangelist, you must sharpen your evangelistic eyes. Begin by looking for people going through a crisis. As we already discussed, individuals experiencing difficult times are often open to the gospel. Life has placed them in a tough situation. Anxiety levels begin to soar as they desperately search for answers. That is a perfect time to introduce them to the gospel of Christ.

Do you remember the story of Jack from chapter 6? He was troubled by a difficult home situation. Though he tried to find a solution, he only ended up frustrated and hopeless. But then a "friend" shared the story of Jesus. It was the right message at the right time. Jack needed help and, from a trusted friend, openly received the gospel. Jack's experience can be illustrated a thousand times over. People are more receptive to the gospel during times of high stress.

You must understand this principle. Learn to recognize stress and anxiety in your non-Christian friends. Draw close and you will know when difficulty comes. It is common for friends to share problems, looking for help and understanding. Jesus is the greatest help you could possibly offer. Take the step of faith and confidently tell your friends about Him. You will find hurting people open, perhaps more responsive than you thought possible. Do you know a friend in crisis? Can you "see" the evangelistic opportunity?

As a friendship evangelist, you must also "see" open doors when you are in conversation with non-Christians. Something you say or something about the way you live will cause questions to arise in their minds. They may ask about these matters immediately, or they may ponder the matter for a while. But sooner or later they will state their questions. If you recognize the situation, it can be a good opportunity to communicate Christ.

Take John, for example. He works at a local power company in the training division. John was recently equipped in friendship evangelism and is building a relationship with a fellow worker. John's life is different, causing his friend to wonder, "Why is John like this? Is he religious or just unique?" Over time John's friend discovers that he attends church, regularly comments on his faith and even goes to a Bible study in the middle of the week. Sooner or later, under the conviction of the Spirit, that man will ask John an important question or make a comment. Maybe he will ask, "John, why do you go to church so much?" or "Do you really believe all that religious stuff?" If John has evangelistic eyes, he will be able to see a perfect opportunity to share Christ.

Would you have recognized the open door to proclaim the message of salvation? Or would you likely ignore it or answer with only a brief comment? As a friendship evangelist you must look for opportunities to clearly and sensitively share the story of Jesus. If your friend seems to become resistant or uncomfortable, just politely back off. The Lord will continue to convict and convince him or her through the Holy Spirit. But more often than not, you will find that questions signal the person's readiness to hear the gospel.

Do you have evangelistic eyes? Ask the Lord to help you see opportunities for witnessing. Crisis situations, regardless of the intensity, provide fertile soil for evangelism. Remember, people in need are often receptive to the gospel. Likewise, look for open doors when speaking with your friends. Sooner or later those doors will unlock, and when they do, confidently tell your friends about Jesus.

Know where to begin

My family and I attend the Church of the Crossroads in Nanuet, New York. It is a Christian and

Missionary Alliance church started just over two years ago. Several Christians felt a burden for the town of Nanuet. With help from denominational leadership, they called a pastor and began laying the foundation for a new church. The core group decided to officially begin the church on Easter Sunday. They rented a hall and for weeks prepared for the first service. Over 20,000 invitations were sent to area residents. The flyer announced the time of the service, the meeting place and extended a welcome to all visitors. On Easter Sunday 220 people arrived for the first service, and a new church was born!

The pastor wanted all visitors followed up that week. He divided up the names among the core group, asking each one of us to make contact with our list of people before the next week's service. We were instructed to thank the visitors for attending, ask if there were any needs or questions and invite them back.

One afternoon that next week, I visited three different homes in the area. As instructed, I thanked people for attending our church and asked for their impressions and reactions. Before inviting them to return, I asked, "Do you have any questions about God, the morning message or religion in general, that I may be able to answer?" Responses were interesting and revealed an evangelistic principle. When it comes to the gospel, not all non-Christians are at the same level of understanding. One woman was a Buddist and knew nothing about Jesus or the gospel. A second person occasionally attended church, heard of Jesus as Savior, but had no personal relationship with Christ. At the last home I found a young wife who at one time had accepted the Lord as her personal Savior. For years she had not attended church, and she desperately needed help.

Professor James F. Engel, communication specialist at Wheaton College, believes that people vary in their understanding of God and the Christian faith. Evangelists need to be sensitive to this, find out how much people know and build from there.

As an evangelist you must identify where people are in relation to Christ. Once that is determined, seek to move them toward Him and His church. You do this through proclamation and persuasion. Simultaneously the Holy Spirit convicts, regenerates and sanctifies the person as he or she grows in understanding and decides to act. The evangelistic process is not complete until the new convert is incorporated into the church and begins to grow in the Lord.

Just how do you determine a non-Christian's level of understanding? Once the door has opened to talk about the Lord, ask questions. "Do you believe in God?" "Have you ever heard the story of Jesus Christ?" "What would a person need to do if he or she wanted to go to heaven?" Answers to these and other specific questions speak volumes about a person's perceptions of God and knowledge of the Lord. Also, be sensitive to the questions that person asks you. One secular ad says, "Inquiring minds want to know." Once the Holy Spirit begins to work in a person, he or she will search for answers. Their questions will be your lead. Begin where people are and take them to faith in Christ.

It is critically important that you, as a friendship evangelist, follow this principle. Know where to begin and how to lead a person from ignorance to

involvement. If you do, you will find yourself ready
and able to help your non-Christian friends along
the path toward Jesus Christ.

Develop your personal testimony

The most effective way to communicate Christ's
story is through your story. Non-Christians want
to know that the gospel message is real and that
it works. This happens best when lay Christians
clearly and concisely tell about their own experience
of Jesus. People need to hear from everyday disciples, learning firsthand how Jesus changes lives.
Such testimonies of God's grace attract people to the
Lord.

Jim Short was a faithful member of his local
church. He was easygoing, pleasant and fairly satisfied with life. Jim knew the gospel, but he had never
responded personally to the claims of Jesus Christ.
Church was just a routine, and he preferred that
level of commitment.

Harold Collins went to the same church. He was
deeply committed to the Lord and excited about
evangelism. Harold belonged to a ministry called
Christian Businessmen's Committee. CBC was an
interdenominational evangelistic organization,
dedicated to winning businessmen to Christ. They
regularly sponsored invitational luncheons where
Christian businessmen gave their testimonies. Over
the years literally hundreds of men came to Christ at
these meetings.

Harold asked Jim to attend a CBC luncheon one
month, and he accepted. After the meal, a Christian
salesman told about his personal experience of
Christ. Jim was gripped as the man detailed his life

before knowing the Lord. He could identify with him in many ways. The salesman spoke of a hidden emptiness, a deep void that nothing could fill. He then told the audience about Jesus, about sin and about everlasting life. Every step toward Christ was described in a personal way. The message ended with an appeal for all the men present to receive the Lord.

For the first time Jim Short truly heard the gospel. The message broke through every barrier and touched his heart. Why? Because Jim heard Christ's story through another man's story. He was able to identify with the salesman's life. Jim saw that Jesus makes a real difference, one he desperately needed. Today Jim Short is a deeply committed Christian. And the key that unlocked it all for him was a personal testimony.

Take the time to carefully develop your testimony. By following four simple guidelines, you can make your testimony clear, to the point and genuinely evangelistic. It can be easily remembered, always there when you have the opportunity to tell it to a friend. It can be as short as 500 words or less.

First, begin your personal testimony by describing what your life was like before you accepted Jesus Christ. Immediately let me raise a caution flag—*do not dwell on specific sins or drag people through the mud.* Many personal stories misfire at this point. Christians can get so detailed that all the unbeliever hears about is sex, drugs or violence. As one man said after hearing such an account, ''I wasn't sure if he was testifying or bragging.'' Instead, speak in general terms about life before Christ. Feel free to describe such feelings as loneliness, fear, rebellion, emptiness. The non-Christian can identify with those feelings, saying, "That's exactly where I am."

Second, describe how you came to recognize that Jesus was who you needed. In my case, I saw in two Christian men a peace and a happiness I did not have. They lived on top of their problems, while I was always weighed down. Their lives seemed to be purposeful, while mine was misdirected and aimless. I wanted desperately to experience life as they were living it. And the more I watched their lives, the clearer the solution became—Jesus. Maybe a friend told you about the Lord, took you to church or introduced you to his or her pastor. However it happened, share the basic details in your testimony. Again, it will help that person identify with you, recognizing a similar process taking place in his or her life.

Third, and most important, outline the specific steps you took to receive Christ. What you are actually doing is sharing the gospel in the context of your own life. Talk about how you discovered that God had a wonderful plan for your life. Use Scriptures that detail this, reading them to your non-Christian friend. Better yet, let the person read the passages for him or herself. Move on in the same way to talk about sin, the redemptive work of the Lord and the necessary response of commitment. In each case make it personal, scriptural and Christ-centered. Later on in the chapter, we will discuss gospel outlines. They can be a tremendous help at this stage in the personal testimony. Remember to be clear, for you are pointing the way to Christ for a lost and broken person.

Finally, detail the changes that have occurred in

your life since receiving the Lord. As stated previously, non-Christians do not receive Christ because the message sounds true. They are most concerned that it is real and relevant. Your personal story is the best witness to this fact. Tell it! Honestly admit that receiving Christ did not usher you into immediate utopia. Admit that you still have some struggles. But also tell how as a Christian you found great joy, peace, forgiveness and purpose in Christ, how life has taken on new meaning, strength and fulfillment. Your non-Christian friend must hear about the difference Jesus has made in your life. This step in your testimony completes the pilgrimage to Christ.

Your story is the best way to tell His story. Work hard at outlining your personal testimony. It will serve the Lord well. Once you have written the testimony, share it with a Christian friend. Ask for suggestions and make necessary changes. Remember the standard is clarity and conciseness. After reworking it, begin to familiarize yourself with the flow, the details and the Scriptures you are using. Do this until it becomes a permanent resident of your mind and heart. When that happens, you will always be equipped for outreach as God's friendship evangelist.

Watch your language!

One evening two students made a trip to New York City to do street witnessing. They were burdened for the millions of people there who are lost and broken. Backed by prayer and armed with tracts, they journeyed into the "Big Apple." It is not easy to start a conversation with passersby on the streets of

New York. Thousands of people walk quickly, suspicious of each other, hoping for an uninterrupted passage. The two young men were somewhat disappointed, since most people did not accept their tract. Those who did simply took the leaflet and walked on by. Finally after some time a fellow received the tract and asked, "What is this?" Immediately one of the young evangelists sprang into action, answering his question with yet another question. "Have you been washed in the blood of Christ?" With a startled look, the fellow excused himself and quickly walked away.

I can only imagine what the fellow was thinking when he darted away. On the streets of New York City, any mention of blood does not conjure up good images! Even though the evangelists felt their message was positive, to a non-Christian their words were frightening. The young men failed to recognize that Christian language is not easily understood and that it is often misunderstood by those outside Christianity. Too often believers spew out theological terms as if they were part of everyone's daily vocabulary. When this happens, believers fail to adequately communicate the gospel. The language of faith does not match the language of the people.

Consider the following terms and phrases:

Assurance of salvation	Eternal life
Repentance	Born again
Holiness	Sanctification
Convert	Justification
Sin	Disciple
Lost	Spiritual

To Christians each word and phrase is full of mean-

ing. But to non-Christians each is either ambiguous
or meaningless. If friendship evangelists use these
terms, they may not communicate. We must be careful to choose words or phrases that have meaning to
non-Christians or to define the terms we do use.

John Wesley, the founder of Methodism, had an
interesting way to prepare for preaching. After writing a sermon, he would often share it with his maid.
He asked her to identify any words or phrases that
she did not understand. By doing this, Wesley in-
sured that his sermon was clear to the common person. Our commitment should be precisely the same.
We must watch our words, making sure the message
of Jesus is truly spoken in the language of the
people.

Learn to use a gospel outline

In chapter 1 we discussed the nature of biblical
evangelism. Our definition emphasized four necessary ingredients if outreach is going to be effective:
presence, proclamation, persuasion and power. Gospel outlines can keep you on track in the second area
of evangelism—proclamation. They will help you lay
out the basic elements of the gospel message. And
they keep your presentation clear, systematic and
responsible. Outlines move both you and your listener step-by-step toward your goal of achieving a
responsible decision for Jesus Christ. When used
properly, they can be a wonderful tool in your
evangelism.

Here are several of the better gospel outlines. Notice that in one way or another, each deals with the
basic ingredients of the gospel. (See chapter 2,
"Chosen as His Messenger").

The Roman Road

Humanity's sin: **Romans 3:23**, "For all have sinned and fall short of the glory of God."

Sin's penalty: **Romans 6:23**, "For the wages of sin is death, but the gift of God is eternal life in Christ Jesus our Lord."

God's provision: **Romans 5:8**, "But God demonstrates his own love for us in this: While we were still sinners, Christ died for us."

Humanity's response of faith: **Romans 10:9**, "That if you confess with your mouth, 'Jesus is Lord,' and believe in your heart that God raised him from the dead, you will be saved."

Humanity's response of commitment: **Romans 12:1–2**, "Therefore, I urge you, brothers, in view of God's mercy, to offer your bodies as living sacrifices, holy and pleasing to God—this is your spiritual act of worship. Do not conform any longer to the pattern of this world, but be transformed by the renewing of your mind. Then you will be able to test and approve what God's will is—his good, pleasing and perfect will."

The Gospel of John

God's purpose: **John 1:1–3**, "In the beginning was the Word, and the Word was with God, and the Word was God. He was with God in the beginning. Through him all things were made; without him nothing was made that has been made."

Humanity's need: **John 3:3**, "In reply Jesus declared, 'I tell you the truth, no one can see the kingdom of God unless he is born again.'"

God's provision: **John 1:14, John 3:16,** "The
Word became flesh and made his dwelling
among us. We have seen his glory, the glory of
the One and Only, who came from the Father,
full of grace and truth." "For God so loved the
world that he gave his one and only Son, that
whoever believes in him shall not perish but have
eternal life."

Humanity's response: **John 1:12, John 3:36,** "Yet
to all who received him, to those who believed in
his name, he gave the right to become children
of God." "Whoever believes in the Son has eternal life, but whoever rejects the Son will not see
life, for God's wrath remains on him."

Steps to Peace with God

God's plan—peace and life
God loves you and wants you to experience
peace and life—abundant and eternal (John
10:10).

Since God planned for us to have peace and the
abundant life right now, why are most people
not having this experience?

Acknowledge man's problem—separation
Man chose to disobey God and still makes that
choice today. This results in *separation* from God
(Romans 3:23).

God's remedy—the cross
Jesus Christ is the only answer to the problem of
separation. He paid the penalty for our sin and
made it possible to be reunited with God (John
14:6).

Man's response—receive Christ
We must trust Jesus Christ and receive Him into

our hearts. Christ speaks to us, asking to enter our lives as our personal Savior and Lord (Revelation 3:20).

Is there any good reason why you cannot receive Jesus Christ right now?[40]

How to Find God

Turn—repent of sinful life and turn to Christ.

Trust—Jesus Christ as your personal Savior and Lord.

Take—the free gift of redemption offered by God.

Thank—Jesus for saving you, taking Him at His word.

Tell—share your experiences and new life with someone else.[41]

Four Things You Want to Know

Your need as God sees it:

Romans 3:23 "For all have sinned and fall short of the glory of God."

Romans 3:10, 11 "As it is written: / 'There is no one righteous, not even one; / there is no one who understands, / no one who seeks God.'"

Jeremiah 17:9 "The heart is deceitful above all things / and beyond cure. / Who can understand it?"

Isaiah 64:6 "All of us have become like one who is unclean, / and all our righteous acts are like filthy rags; / we all shrivel up like a leaf, / and like the wind our sins sweep us away."

John 3:3 "In reply Jesus declared, 'I tell you the truth, no one can see the kingdom of God unless he is born again.'"

Your own helplessness:

John 14:6 "Jesus answered, 'I am the way and the truth and the life. No one comes to the Father except through me.' "

Acts 4:12 "Salvation is found in no one else, for there is no other name under heaven given to men by which we must be saved."

Galatians 2:16 " . . . a man is not justified by observing the law, but by faith in Jesus Christ. So we, too, have put our faith in Christ Jesus that we may be justified by faith in Christ and not by observing the law, because by observing the law no one will be justified."

James 2:10 "For whoever keeps the whole law and yet stumbles at just one point is guilty of breaking all of it."

Proverbs 14:12 "There is a way that seems right to a man, / but in the end it leads to death."

God's provision for your need:

John 3:16 "For God so loved the world that he gave his one and only Son, that whoever believes in him shall not perish but have eternal life."

Isaiah 53:6 "We all, like sheep, have gone astray, / each of us has turned to his own way; / and the Lord has laid on him / the iniquity of us all."

2 Corinthians 5:21 "God made him who had no sin to be sin for us, so that in him we might become the righteousness of God."

1 Peter 3:18 "For Christ died for sins once for all, the righteous for the unrighteous, to bring you to God. He was put to death in the body but made alive by the Spirit."

God's promise to meet your need:

John 10:28 "I give them eternal life, and they shall never perish; no one can snatch them out of my hand."

Philippians 1:6 "Being confident of this, that he who began a good work in you will carry it on to completion until the day of Christ Jesus."

Hebrews 7:25 "Therefore he is able to save completely those who come to God through him, because he always lives to intercede for them."

Jude 24-25 "To him who is able to keep you from falling and to present you before his glorious presence without fault and with great joy—to the only God our Savior be glory, majesty, power and authority, through Jesus Christ our Lord, before all ages, now and forevermore! Amen."

Therefore:

Change your attitude toward sin—**Acts 3:19** "Repent, then, and turn to God, so that your sins may be wiped out, that times of refreshing may come from the Lord."

Put your trust in Jesus Christ—**Acts 16:31** "They replied, 'Believe in the Lord Jesus, and you will be saved—you and your household.' "[42]

You should become familiar with one or more of these outlines. It may be helpful to carry a copy with you as a guide when sharing Christ. It is best to know the outline and the Scriptures by memory, putting the basic message into your own words. This will keep the presentation personal, yet biblically systematic and balanced. When giving your testi-

mony or simply sharing the gospel, the outline helps
you move a person toward a decision. It is particularly effective to have the other person read these
verses from your Bible. As you share the main
points, open the Word to supporting Scriptures and
let him or her read them aloud. This will reinforce
the accuracy of your testimony, adding the powerful
authority of God's Word.

I do need to sound a warning about gospel outlines. Used improperly, they can become impersonal
and mechanical. Remember that every person is
unique. If you force-feed the same approach, without interruption, evangelism becomes stiff. Worse,
you might begin to trust the technique more than
the power of God and the leading of His Holy Spirit.
Remember, the outline is a tool, not a technique—a
guide, not the complete gospel. But properly used,
the gospel outline can help you reap a harvest of
lives for the Lord.

The final step: commitment

The final step in leading a person to Christ is no
easier than the first. More than once I have received
calls from lay evangelists asking for help. It often
goes something like this: "Terry, I've been sharing
the gospel with my friend Bill. He is open and wants
to give his life to Christ. Would you please come
over, talk with him and help him receive the Lord?"
For some reason, friendship evangelists are often apprehensive or unsure about this climactic stage in
evangelism. So that you will not be in a fog at this
critical moment, consider these suggestions.

First, after you have clearly shared the gospel, ask
if there are any questions. Be sure your friend under-

stands the content and implications of the good news. You do not want him or her to respond prematurely or without clarity of mind. Normally there will be points you need to rehearse. Be careful, though, not to be sidetracked. If your friend's question deals with an unrelated topic, politely, yet definitely, keep to the main issues of the gospel. If there are no questions, quickly restate the primary points of the outline as a final summary.

Second, once you are confident that your friend understands, ask him or her to receive the Lord. "John/Mary, do you want to receive Jesus into your life right now?" You may feel apprehensive, but step out in faith, asking the Holy Spirit to be your guide. If the response is "no," try to discover why. There may be a barrier that you can help remove. If the response is, "I just need more time," politely remind the person of the urgency of this matter. But do not persist. Encourage your friend to take a day or two to think about it. I always tell people two things at this point. First, "If you find you want to surrender your life to Christ before I see you again, feel free to call me. I'll be glad to meet with you and help." Second, "Here is a prayer that will help if you find you just can't wait. The Lord will be there, and He will hear and come into your heart." At that point I write out a short prayer as a guide and give it to the person.

If your friend responds "yes," guide him or her in asking Christ into his or her heart. I simply remind people that it is a step of faith, done through prayer. And I suggest that if they are willing, I could lead them. Usually non-Christians agree, so I pray aloud, asking the person to sincerely repeat each line. The following prayer serves as a guide, much the same as a gospel outline.

> Dear Father in heaven, I come to You today, in faith, believing that You hear this prayer. You have a wonderful plan and purpose for my life. But I am a sinner. I have been living my own way, far from You. Right now, I repent of my sin and receive Jesus Christ, Your Son, as my Savior. I believe that He died for my sin and that He wants to give me new life. I also surrender myself to Christ's Lordship, committing myself to follow Him. I thank You for giving me salvation by Your grace, through faith. Amen.

Notice that the four basic elements of the gospel are woven into this prayer. Under the Holy Spirit's guidance, it helps a person honestly and sincerely surrender to the Lord.

Finally, rejoice with your new brother or sister, assuring him or her that Christ has heard and answered. Encourage your friend not to dwell on feelings, though they may be real. Take him or her immediately to the facts in God's Word. Share passages such as,

> Yet to all who received him, to those who believed in his name, he gave the right to become children of God. (John 1:12)
> If you confess with your mouth, ''Jesus is Lord,'' and believe in your heart that God raised him from the dead, you will be saved. (Romans 10:9)
> Anyone who believes in the Son of God has this testimony in his heart. . . . And this is the testimony: God has given us eternal life, and this life is in his Son. (1 John 5:10a, 11)

I often go to Luke 15 and the parable of the lost sheep. There, Scripture emphasizes great rejoicing when one sinner repents. I tell my new brother or sister that his or her repentance has brought joy to God and all who belong to Him. Once you bring a person to this point, it is time to begin follow-up. That is the focus of the next chapter.

Finish with Follow-Up

A REA CHURCHES RECEIVED repeated announcements that youth meetings would be held at Pittsburgh's Syria Mosque. A well-known Christian leader was coming for seven nights of evangelistic meetings. Organizers energetically promoted the event, hoping hundreds would attend. Local congregations mobilized their youth groups, instructing teens to invite unsaved friends and relatives. People activated prayer groups, rented buses and made other preparations—all focused on seven special nights.

John Glass and Barry Carter did not regularly attend church. Though they had never met, both came to the crusade for one of the evening services. They were from separate areas of the city, invited by different youth groups. The speaker delivered a powerful sermon that night, aimed directly at teenagers. At the close of the meeting, John and Barry went forward to give their hearts to Christ. They were equally touched and sincere.

John Glass was immediately asked to become part of a local youth program. Counselors and sponsors took a special interest in him, providing transportation to church services and teen events. One older

Christian befriended John, spending time teaching him the basics of Christian discipleship. Within a year John Glass was an active part of the church and a faithful Christian. Since then he has gone on to win numerous people to Christ.

Barry Carter was also deeply moved by the message. Standing near the platform at the end of the service, he committed his life to Jesus Christ. Words could not express the joy and excitement he felt that night. He rode home with dozens of teens packed into a rented school bus. He did not know anyone there, but he felt safe as he reflected on his new faith. For several days Barry regularly read the Bible. While he did not understand everything, its truths brought comfort and direction. But as so often happens, the demands of an ungodly world cried out for his attention. He tried as best he could to keep his eyes on Christ. Barry even considered attending youth meetings at the local church—but he did not. And within a few short months, that special evening was but a memory. Life was the same as it had been before.

I heard this story from John Glass. He was attending a retreat in the Pennsylvania mountains, where I was the weekend speaker. John met Barry Carter through a common friend several years after the Pittsburgh event. By what seemed to be a coincidence, it was discovered that they both had attended the crusade. John told me about Barry following a lecture I gave on the importance of follow-up.

I have come to this conclusion: Leading a person to Christ is important, but how that person is followed up after conversion is even more critical. After-care determines the ongoing faithfulness of a new convert. When follow-up is consistent, people most often move on to discipleship. When it is weak or nonexistent, new believers will likely fall away, due to spiritual malnutrition.

Let us not forget the true goal of evangelism. Jesus commanded His followers to make *disciples*, not *decisions*. When you lead a person to Christ, you have an obligation to insure quality follow-up. Just like biological parents care for newborn babies, so as a spiritual "parent" you must be committed to follow-up. Newborn Christians need special attention, lots of love and regular meals from God's Word.

How does follow-up usually happen?

Healthy local churches are committed to follow-up for new believers. Normally this happens in any one of several ways. First, churches often have a new believers' class. New converts are encouraged to join with other young Christians for study and support. Our church has such a program, offered four times a year. The class meets weekly for three months, with 10–12 lessons. Topics range from assurance of salvation to witnessing, rooting the new believer in Christ.

Second, many local churches organize one-to-one discipleship programs. An older, mature believer agrees to meet regularly with a new convert. Normal programs run one to two hours a week for up to three months. Similar to new believers' classes, each session focuses on a topic basic to spiritual growth. One-to-one discipleship programs are especially effective because of personalized care. Lasting relationships often develop, much like that of Paul and Timothy spoken of in Scripture.

Third, several churches do follow-up through their small group program. New believers are placed into existing small groups for study and fellowship. This quickly assimilates people into the life of a local church. Young Christians are able to meet other members of the church, developing a deep sense of belonging. There is, though, a serious disadvantage. Subject matter is not always basic enough for "babes in Christ." Yet the bond of fellowship is generally strong enough to keep converts coming back.

As a friendship evangelist, you need to help new believers get involved in follow-up. Find out about your local church after-care program. Then, either take your friend to the first meeting, or introduce him or her to those in charge. Your relationship will serve as a powerful bridge that links conversion with discipleship. Take a personal interest, insuring that your special brother or sister does not get lost in the follow-up gap. Encourage the person in every way possible, remembering that all eternity is at stake.

When it is up to you!

Unfortunately, not all churches have follow-up programs for new believers. If that is true in your church, be prepared to provide the necessary after-care yourself. You are responsible to personally nurture your friend in Christ. The prospect may seem overwhelming, yet you must accept the challenge. Your friend is too precious to God and to you to neglect follow-up. If properly prepared, you will find that the experience will strengthen your own faith as well.

What follows is a 12-lesson follow-up program. Let it be your guide in leading your friend to responsible discipleship. It is a basic introduction to the Christian faith. Each lesson focuses on one important aspect of discipleship. Meet weekly for 60–90 minutes, covering the questions and assignments contained in each lesson. As leader, take adequate time to pray and prepare before each meeting. Review all material and Scripture verses well in advance, adding information and insights as needed.

You should ask your friend to commit him or herself to follow-up. If your friendship is already well established, that should not be difficult. Carefully emphasize its importance. Clearly communicate that spiritual growth is required of Christ's disciples, sharing Colossians 2:6–7 as a challenge: "So then, just as you received Christ Jesus as Lord, continue to live in him, rooted and built up in him, strengthened in the faith as you were taught, and overflowing with thankfulness."

Once the new convert agrees, I suggest doing four things:

> Pray, committing each other to the follow-up program.
> Agree to read John 1 and 2 for the next week.
> Ask your friend to write out any questions or doubts he or she may have.
> Memorize Second Corinthians 5:17.

From there, agree on a good meeting time and get ready for an incredible three-month journey in faith!

Lesson 1—New Life in Christ

Welcome to the greatest family in the universe— God's family! By receiving the Lord Jesus Christ into your heart, God has adopted you as one of His children. You are now the heir to special rights and privileges reserved for God's children. His promises have been revealed in the pages of Scripture. Today, we will focus on some of the exciting assurances God has given you.

Let's review: Take a few minutes to look back at what happened to you last week.

1. Let's review the gospel message using one of the gospel outlines provided in this book.

2. Were you sincere when you asked Christ into your heart?

3. Have you turned away from sin and toward obedience to Christ?

4. Do you believe that God lives within you?

5. What evidences are there that you have been born again?

6. Do you have any doubts or questions?

Let's move on: Today we will focus upon several key promises God has given His children.

1. You now have eternal life. (1 John 5:11–13)

2. You are a new creation in Christ Jesus. (2 Corinthians 5:17)

3. You have been adopted into God's family. (Ephesians 1:3–6)

4. You have been saved by grace through faith. (Ephesians 2:8–10)

5. Jesus paid the penalty for your sin. (Colossians 2:13–15)

6. God's Spirit will confirm that you belong to Him. (Romans 8:16)

7. God's Spirit will be your constant help. (John 15:13)

8. Nothing will separate you from God's love. (Romans 8:35–39)
9. You can have victory over sin. (1 John 5:5)
10. You now have peace with God. (Romans 5:1)

Let's discuss these 10 points.

Let's prepare for next week:
Scripture reading—John 3–4
Scripture memorization—John 15:10
Write out any questions or doubts.

Lesson 2—Jesus Christ Is Lord

A Christian leader once noted that evangelism in the United States calls many people to faith, but few to obedience. Too often individuals want Christ's salvation, yet they live their lives by the world's standards. True discipleship involves both surrender and obedience. Jesus is Lord and we must say yes to His commands. Christians are called to follow His teaching and example in all they do. Today let us discuss Jesus Christ as Lord.

Let's review: Take a few minutes to look back at the promises God gives to His children.
1. How can you know for sure that Christ is in your heart? (Romans 8:16)
2. What did Jesus do for you on the cross? (Colossians 2:13–15)
3. How secure are you in God's family? (Romans 8:35–39)
4. How did you receive peace with God? (Romans 5:1)
5. What is the role of the Comforter (God's Spirit)? (John 15:13)

6. Do you have any questions or doubts?

Let's move on: Today we will consider the relationship believers should have to Jesus Christ, the Lord.

1. What name did God give Christ Jesus? (Philippians 2:11)

2. What two actions will people take because Jesus is Lord?
   a. Philippians 2:10
   b. Philippians 2:11

3. What do these two actions signify?

4. Why did Jesus question those who called him Lord? (Luke 6:46)

5. Can you identify the Lordship principles found in these verses?
   a. Luke 14:26
   b. Luke 15:33
   c. John 15:9-10
   d. John 14:15
   e. John 14:21

6. How are we to view work as Christians? (Colossians 3:23-24)

7. What should be our attitude before the Lord? (James 4:10)

Let's discuss these seven points.

Let's prepare for next week:
   Scripture reading—John 5-6
   Scripture memorization—Luke 11:9-10
   Write out any questions or doubts.

Lesson 3—Learning to Pray

The Lord invites His children to regularly communicate with Him through prayer. We can have constant access to God, lifting all burdens and problems before His throne. Prayer puts believers in touch with the resources of heaven for power, protection and provision. As we pray, our relationship with Christ grows ever stronger. Together, let us learn to pray as God's Word teaches.

Let's review: Look back to last week's lesson on the Lordship of Jesus Christ.

1. List any specific ways in which you have submitted to Christ's Lordship.

2. How could you make Jesus Lord of your possessions?

3. Are there areas of your life in which you struggle to make Christ Lord? List them and then pray about them.

4. Why do you think Jesus links obedience to love?

5. What does the following statement mean to you? "If Jesus is not Lord of all, He is not Lord at all."

6. Do you have any questions or doubts?

Let's move on: Our focus today will be on the power of prayer.

1. Notice the pattern prayer Jesus taught His disciples in Luke 11:1–4:

    a. praise/worship

    b. pray for God's will in your life and in the lives of others

    c. surrender daily needs to Him

    d. confess sin and repent

    e. trust God for help in trial and temptation

2. What principle of prayer is found in Luke 11:5–10?

3. What condition does Jesus attach to answered prayer? (John 15:7)

4. The following Scriptures tell us when to pray:
   a. Mark 1:35
   b. 1 Thessalonians 5:17
   c. Philippians 4:6
   d. James 5:13-16
   e. Ephesians 6:18

5. Notice that these Scriptures tell us what to pray for:
   a. Luke 22:40
   b. Luke 6:28
   c. Colossians 4:3
   d. Colossians 1:10
   e. Ephesians 1:18

Let's discuss the above five points.

Let's prepare for next week:
Scripture reading—John 7-8
Scripture memorization—1 Corinthians 10:13
Write out any questions or doubts.

Lesson 4—Overcoming Temptation

Satan is not pleased that you have become a follower of Jesus Christ. He will use anything and everything to entice you back to a life of sin. It is critically important that you learn to recognize and overcome the enemy. Jesus Christ has defeated Satan and will empower you to walk in victory! Let's learn the keys to overcoming temptation.

Let's review: How have you progressed in prayer over the past week?

1. Have you spent quality time in prayer using the outline from Luke 11:1–4? Was it helpful?
2. What specific needs did you lift before God?
3. Did you experience any answers to prayer?
4. When was the best time for you to pray each day?
5. How did prayer help you in times of temptation? (Luke 22:40)
6. Do you have any questions or doubts?

Let's move on: Christians are engaged in a mighty battle and must learn to overcome the temptations of Satan.
1. Notice what Paul says about our struggle against Satan in Ephesians 6:10–12.
2. What five pieces of armor must we wear to fight him? (Ephesians 6:9–17)
   a. belt of truth
   b. breastplate of righteousness
   c. shoes of readiness of the gospel
   d. shield of faith
   e. sword of the Spirit
3. What confidence can we have when facing temptation?
   a. 1 Corinthians 10:13
   b. 1 John 4:4
4. Why is Jesus particularly sympathetic with us about temptation? (Hebrews 4:15)
5. In what three areas does Satan most often tempt us? (1 John 2:16)
6. Notice the stance Christians should take toward the devil (James 4:7)
7. Read Luke 4:1–13. The following principles of fighting Satan are revealed in this passage.

a. Satan tempts with lust of the eyes, lust of the flesh and pride of life

b. do not submit to his lies

c. use the Word of God as a defense

8. What does Colossians 2:15 say about Satan? Remember this always.

9. Reflect on the promise of Revelation 12:10–12.

Let's discuss the above nine points.

Let's prepare for next week:
Scripture reading—John 9–10
Scripture memorization—2 Timothy 3:16
Write out any questions or doubts.

Lesson 5—Study the Word of God

God has revealed His will for Christians in the pages of the Bible. His Word contains everything we need to know for growing in our faith. In Scripture we discover information about God, ourselves, relationships with others and much, much more. As a young Christian, it is critically important that you learn to read and study the Word of God. You will find that it provides just the right nourishment for growing strong in Christ.

Let's review: Probably Satan tried to tempt you to sin this past week. Did you stand strong in Christ?

1. In what way did Satan tempt you?

2. Did you follow the advice of James 4:7?

3. Why is Jesus able to help us in times of temptation? (Hebrews 9:15)

4. How well did you hold on to the promise of First Corinthians 10:13?

5. What can you do to eliminate some of the enemy's temptation?

6. Do you have any doubts or questions?

Let's move on: The Bible is God's personal letter to you. Learn to study its instruction each day.

1. Read First Peter 2:2. What does Peter call a new Christian?

2. What should the new Christian long for?

3. Second Timothy 3:16 tells us that God's Word is God-breathed. What do you think that means?

4. What use does Scripture have in the believer's life? (2 Timothy 3:16)

5. What special instructions did God give Joshua regarding His Word? (Joshua 1:6–8)

6. When should God's people read His Word? (Joshua 1:8)

7. Read Psalm 1. What is the key to living a prosperous Christian life?

8. When reading God's Word, consider these four guidelines: read it slowly, systematically, sensitively and sincerely (see chapter 4).

9. What is God's command to you regarding His Word? (2 Timothy 2:15)

Let's discuss the above nine points.

Let's prepare for next week:
Scripture reading—John 11–12
Scripture memorization—Ephesians 4:3
Write out any questions or doubts.

Lesson 6—Fellowship with One Another

Christians should not live isolated from other believers. Instead, they are to develop loving relationships characterized by unity, encouragement and support. Together we can resist the enemy, grow strong in the Lord and boldly witness for Jesus Christ. Our Lord has called believers out of the world and toward one another. We must make a deep commitment to the people of Christ, meeting regularly for fellowship. That will be the focus of this lesson.

Let's review: Scripture is God's inspired Word given to His children.

1. What particular truths did you discover in God's Word this past week?

2. Why is reading the Scriptures so important to Christians?

3. What was God's promised key to success recorded in Joshua 1:7?

4. List again the four purposes of God's Word recorded in Second Timothy 3:16.

5. What equips believers for every good work? (2 Timothy 2:15)

6. Do you have any questions or doubts?

Let's move on: Christians must learn to depend on one another in the body of Christ.

1. What distinguishes Christians as disciples of the Lord Jesus Christ? (John 13:35, 39)

2. Read Hebrews 10:24–25. Note three admonitions given to believers:

   a. spur one another on to love and good deeds

   b. do not give up meeting together

   c. encourage one another

3. What one principle emerges from First Corinthians 12:12–26?

4. Ephesians 4:15–16 emphasizes growing to-

gether in love and growing mature in Christ. Review.

5. What characterized the new believers' commitment to each other in Acts 2:44?

6. What responsibility do Christians have for one another? (Romans 15:1–2)

7. Read Ecclesiastes 4:9–12 and discuss why two people are better than one.

8. What should Christians do when they meet together? (Colossians 3:15–16; Acts 2:42–47)

9. List the times and places that you meet with other Christians for the above activities.

Let's discuss the above nine points.

Let's prepare for next week:
Scripture reading—John 13–14
Scripture memorization—Hebrews 13:15
Write out any questions or doubts.

Lesson 7—The Role of the Holy Spirit

Before Jesus ascended into heaven He told His disciples to wait in Jerusalem for the Holy Spirit. Our Lord did not want His followers to face life and ministry alone. He promised to send His Spirit, known to believers as the Helper and the Comforter. God's Spirit is still at work, wanting to infill and empower believers. Today we will focus on the role of the Holy Spirit in your life.

Let's review: Christians do not only enter into a relationship with Christ, but they are bonded together with every other Christian. The Bible calls us the body of Christ.

1. Today, in review, reflect upon these "one another" passages that are found in God's Word.

accept one another
bear one another's burdens
care for one another
comfort one another
confess your sins to one another
serve one another
show patience to one another
be hospitable toward each other
be kind to one another
love one another
pray for one another
be at peace with one another
encourage one another
fellowship with one another
forgive one another

2. What do these admonitions tell you about our commitment to other Christian believers?

3. Do you have any doubts or questions?

Let's move on: The Holy Spirit is God's provision for growth, protection and fruitfulness.

1. What do these Scriptures tell you about the Holy Spirit?
   a. Genesis 1:2
   b. Romans 8:14
   c. John 14:16–17
   d. Romans 1:4
   e. John 16:8
   f. Matthew 3:16

2. When does the Holy Spirit come to the believer? (Ephesians 1:13)

3. What must a person do to receive the Holy Spirit? (Ephesians 1:13)

4. Jesus tells us that the Holy Spirit comes to do certain things in our lives. What two activities does He mention in John 14:26?

5. Where does the Holy Spirit take up residence in your life? (John 14:17)

6. Read what Jesus says about how long the Holy Spirit will be with you. (John 14:16)

7. What four things does the Holy Spirit want to do in you?

   a. John 14:17

   b. 2 Thessalonians 2:13 and Hebrews 9:14

   c. 1 Corinthians 12:11 (also read 1 Corinthians 12:1–11)

   d. Acts 1:8

8. God gives specific guidance on how to receive the Spirit's fullness. What is it? (Luke 11:13)

Let's discuss the above eight points.

Let's prepare for next week:
   Scripture reading—John 15–16
   Scripture memorization—Proverbs 3:5–6
   Write out any questions or doubts.

Lesson 8—God Has a Will for Your Life

A common question Christians ask is, "How can I know God's will for my life?" We are constantly faced with decisions and must know how to best determine God's plan. Be assured that the Heavenly Father wants you to know His will. He does not want you to decide in the dark or make wrong choices. Today we will look at God's promises and consider some practical steps toward discovering His will.

Let's review: The Holy Spirit of God is actively at work in your life. Have you recognized His presence?

1. Has the Holy Spirit helped you in any way this past week?

2. What two sins does God's Word warn us about relative to the Holy Spirit? (1 Thessalonians 5:19; Ephesians 4:30)

3. Review the fruit of the Spirit's presence in you as recorded in Galatians 5:22–25.

4. What particular sins has the Holy Spirit convicted you of in recent days?

5. Do you have any questions or doubts?

Let's move on: Scripture reveals that God has a wonderful plan for our lives.

1. The Bible tells us that God wants to guide us into His way. Read Psalm 25:8–10.

2. What is the first key to discovering His will for our lives? (Matthew 6:33)

3. Before seeking direction in specific situations, be sure you are submissive to His general will. What is that will?

    a. 2 Peter 3:9

    b. 1 Thessalonians 4:3

    c. Ephesians 5:17–18.

4. When facing a decision what should you do? (James 1:5)

5. If you seek God's will, He will answer your prayers. Read First John 5:14–15.

6. What is the problem with doing things your own way, without direction from God? (Isaiah 55:8; Joshua 9:1–15)

7. What steps should you take to discover the will of God in your life?

    a. Psalm 119:105—delight in the Word

    b. Proverbs 11:14; 15:22—receive counsel from mature believers

    c. Acts 13:2–3—follow the Holy Spirit's guidance

    d. Proverbs 3:5-6—submit your plans to God
    e. Colossians 1:9—pray
  8. What advice does Paul give in Romans 12:2
about discovering God's will?

Let's discuss the above eight points.

Let's prepare for next week:
  Scripture reading—John 17-18
  Scripture memorization—Matthew 28:18-20
  Write out questions or doubts.

Lesson 9—How to Be an Effective Witness

When Jesus called the first disciples, He said, "Come, follow me, . . . and I will make you fishers of men" (Mark 1:17). From the beginning the Lord made it clear that witnessing was a basic ingredient of discipleship. Every Christian must be ready and willing to share the message of salvation with others. Jesus wants us to reach out to lost men and women everywhere, spreading His good news. Today we will discuss why, how and when we should do that.

Let's review: God wants you to walk daily according to His Word and His will. How have you been doing?
  1. Have you faced any decisions this past week?
  2. How did you arrive at the answers?
  3. Are there any areas in your life presently outside of God's will?
  4. What guidance would you give another person about discovering God's will?
  5. What three adjectives does Paul use when speaking about God's will in Romans 12:2?
  6. Do you have any questions or doubts?

Let's move on: Thousands of people all around you are lost and without Christ. Will you do your part in reaching them?

1. What is God's desire for this lost and broken world? (1 Timothy 2:4)

2. Why are people lost and bound for eternal death? (Romans 3:23; 6:23)

3. What has God done for sinners? (John 3:16; Colossians 2:13–15)

4. How will people find out about God's salvation? (Romans 1:14–15)

5. What name has God given you? (2 Corinthians 5:20)

6. As an ambassador, what should you be doing? (2 Corinthians 5:20)

7. What message has God committed to you? (2 Corinthians 5:19)

8. Read Matthew 28:18–20. What is Christ's command?

9. How is a person saved? (Ephesians 2:8–9)

10. Review the following Scriptures, which outline the gospel message: Romans 3:23; 6:23; 5:8; 10:9; 12:1–2.

11. Who motivates us to faithfully witness? (Acts 1:8)

Let's discuss the above 11 points.

Let's prepare for next week:
Scripture reading—John 19–20
Scripture memorization—John 15:5
Write out any questions or doubts.

Lesson 10—The Quiet Time

The Lord Jesus wants to develop a deep and lasting

relationship with you, His disciple. Just as with any vital relationship, doing that takes time and commitment. The saints of the past set apart time each day to meet with God. They would turn to God in prayer, and He would speak to them through His Word and His Spirit. Their devotional life became a great source of growth and strength. Every believer should prioritize a daily quiet time with God. That will be the focus of this week's lesson.

Let's review: Have you had any opportunities to witness for Christ lately?

1. List the names of at least five non-Christian friends.

2. What is God's greatest desire for their lives?

3. If God opened the door for you to share the gospel, what would you say?

4. How can people receive God's gift of salvation? (Romans 6:23; Ephesians 2:8–9)

5. What is the Great Commission? Where is it found in Scripture?

6. Do you have any doubts or questions?

Let's move on: To grow strong in Christ you must spend quality time with Him in prayer and study.

1. Was quiet time with God important to Jesus? (Mark 1:35)

2. When did He get alone with the Father?

3. What was David's attitude about time with God? (Psalm 63:1)

4. What is the source of fruit in a believer's life? (John 15:5)

5. What thoughts come to mind when Jesus says to abide in Him?

6. Consider these suggestions for having an effec-

tive quiet time:

    a. Ask the Lord to give you a desire to have a quiet time.

    b. Find a suitable place.

    c. Choose your best time.

    d. Develop a simple format. (I suggest the S.T.O.P. plan: **Silence**—begin with quiet stillness before the Lord; **Thankfulness**—praise God for who He is and what He has done; **Openness**—read a section of God's Word, reflecting on its truths; **Prayer**—using an outline such as the Lord's prayer, petition the Heavenly Father.)

    e. Ask a Christian friend to pray for you about having a consistent quiet time.

    7. How should we approach God in our quiet time? (Hebrews 11:6)

Let's discuss the above seven points.

Let's prepare for next week:
    Scripture reading—John 21
    Scripture memorization—1 Peter 2:9–10
    Write out any questions or doubts.

Lesson 11—Getting Involved in a Healthy Church

In Matthew 16:18 the Lord Jesus said, "I will build my church, and the gates of Hades will not overcome it." The word "church" refers to all born-again believers, called out of the world for holiness and called into the world for witness and service. The Bible gives clear teachings on the nature and function of the church. Today we will discuss the characteristics of a healthy church. You should commit to such a body of believers for personal holiness and service.

Let's review: As we discussed last week, every Christian must develop a quality devotional life.

1. Talk about your experience during your quiet time this week.

    a. How often did you meet God in quiet time?

    b. How long did you normally spend in quiet time?

    c. What truths did you glean from Scripture?

    d. What effect did your quiet time have in your life?

2. Who is praying for you regarding your quiet time?

3. Do you have any questions or doubts?

Let's move on: Every Christian should be active in a healthy local church.

1. Who is Head of the church? (Ephesians 5:23)

2. Who is to provide leadership in the local church? (Titus 1:5)

3. What responsibilities do leaders have to the church? (Acts 20:28–31; 1 Peter 5:1–3)

4. How should church members view the leaders of a local church? (Hebrews 13:17; 1 Timothy 5:17)

5. Notice the characteristics of a healthy church. (Acts 2:42–47)

    a. teaching of Scripture

    b. fellowship

    c. communion

    d. generosity

    e. worship

    f. evangelistic growth

6. What is the role of pastors in the church?

(Ephesians 4:12–13)

7. Who is to do the work of ministry in a church? (Ephesians 4:12)

8. Who determines the ministry Christians are to have in a church? (1 Corinthians 12:11)

9. What is the supreme mark of the Christian church? (John 13:34–35)

10. What local church are you attending?

Let's discuss the above 10 points.

Let's prepare for next week:
 Scripture reading—Matthew 25
 Scripture memorization—1 Corinthians 4:2
 Write out any questions or doubts.

Lesson 12—How to Be a Faithful Steward

Our Heavenly Father is generous with His children. He places countless resources at their disposal. But these gifts are not to be hoarded or used solely for selfish desires. Time, talents and finances are not only for our blessing, but also for the blessing of others. As God's child it is critically important that you faithfully give to the Lord's work. Today we will discuss the issue of faithful stewardship.

Let's review: Every believer should be active in a healthy church.

1. Are you regularly involved in a church?
2. Evaluate your church by biblical standards:
 a. Is the Word preached and taught?
 b. Are people friendly and enthusiastic?
 c. Do worship services inspire and instruct you?
 d. Does the church emphasize evangelism?
 e. Is the church growing numerically?

3. List all the ways you are presently involved in the church.

4. Do you have any questions or doubts?

Let's move on: Disciples should serve God with their time, talents and finances.

1. Read Matthew 6:25–33. What does verse 33 teach about the priority of our lives?

2. What does Psalm 24:1 say about the earth and its resources? Does that include your resources?

3. What is the central principle of the parable in Matthew 25:14–30?

4. What does God call the man who buried his talent? (Matthew 25:6)

5. What principle of giving is identified in Malachi 3:8–12 and Luke 6:38?

6. Notice Paul's instructions in Ephesians 5:15–16 regarding time.

7. God expects us to use spiritual gifts for His kingdom. (1 Peter 4:10)

8. What should be the attitude of our service? (2 Corinthians 9:7)

9. Evaluate your stewardship of time, talents, spiritual gifts and finances. Have you been found trustworthy in these areas? (1 Corinthians 4:2)

Let's discuss the above nine points.

We have come to the end of our 12 weeks together in follow-up. Remember, this is not the end of your Christian growth—only the beginning. The Word of God says: "So then, just as you received Christ Jesus as Lord, continue to live in him, rooted and built up in him, strengthened in the faith as you were taught, and overflowing with thankfulness" (Colossians 2:6–7).

Friendship Evangelism and Your Local Church

BEFORE CONCLUDING OUR DISCUSSION of friendship evangelism, please consider one more challenge. *Let God use you to initiate an outreach program in your local church.* Many congregations, large and small, need help in their evangelism ministries. While they may sponsor an occasional outreach emphasis, it is just not enough. Local churches need to have an ongoing evangelism program that continues all through the year. I am convinced that with a little guidance you could influence your church leaders to begin a friendship evangelism ministry. Would you be willing to try?

The following friendship evangelism program is designed for use in the local church. It is divided into seven steps for easy implementation. Prayerfully approach your pastor with the details of this program. Ask him to consider the idea, and then volunteer to help in whatever way possible. Your pastor may already have other plans. If so, be supportive. If not, God may use this strategy to bring in a great harvest for Christ's kingdom.

How to begin a friendship evangelism ministry

Organize a church evangelism committee. Every congregation needs an evangelism committee to serve as the catalyst for all outreach ministries. It should plan and coordinate evangelism programs that reach out to lost people of all ages. Like a spearhead, the evangelism committee should lead the way to God's harvest field. With the Great Commission as its guide, the committee must set its sights on effective disciple-making.

Pastors and church leaders should carefully select committee members. Try to find people of varied ages, gifts and talents. This broad representation enhances balance and at the same time enables even distribution of responsibility. I highly recommend that the pastor participate on the committee as much as possible. His involvement is critical for the success of the program. The key requirement for membership is, of course, a heartbeat for evangelism.

The evangelism committee should be responsible for the program outlined below. It should plan and prepare the congregation for an effective friendship evangelism ministry.

Plan an evangelism awareness month at your church. Most congregations need a heightened awareness and understanding of evangelism. One way to accomplish this is through a month-long Evangelism Awareness program. Focus on both the opportunity and the responsibility Christians have to reach lost men and women for Christ. The committee will want to inform, inspire and involve as many people as possible in friendship evangelism. Plan the emphasis well in advance and try to get every church department to participate. Saturate every Sunday school class, youth meeting and prayer group with the same theme. Also, ask your pastor to preach about outreach and evangelism during the month. He could easily focus on the Great Commission, the evangelistic message, evangelistic motives, making friends for Christ and related themes.

During Evangelism Awareness month, use all media available for promotion. Sunday school classes, small groups, midweek services and bulletin boards should all focus on friendship evangelism.

Receive an evangelistic faith promise at the end of Evangelism Awareness month. For many years Christian and Missionary Alliance churches have received financial faith promises during their missionary conferences. The idea was originated by A.B. Simpson, founder of the denomination. He used the concept to emphasize that supporting missions should be done with complete dependence upon God. A person should not give what he or she could, but rather promise to give by faith, as God directs and supplies.

The faith promise concept can be transferred to friendship evangelism. During the last service of Awareness month, call for a personal commitment to friendship evangelism. Ask people to make an evangelistic faith promise, trusting that God will use them to lead one person to Christ. The card could read like this:

Evangelistic Faith Promise

In dependence upon God, I will endeavor to

lead one person to Christ through friendship
evangelism over the next _____ months.
Date _____ Name _____

Individuals could fill out the card, bringing it forward in the final service as an act of faith and
commitment.

This concept has been well received where used.
One New York church used the idea and at the close
of Awareness month, 160 adults committed themselves to friendship evangelism. Scores of Christians
can be mobilized for effective outreach in the
church.

*Provide training for everyone who is committed to
friendship evangelism.* Inspiring people in evangelism
is not enough. They need adequate preparation and
training. If this does not happen, your friendship
evangelism program will end before it ever gets
started. As soon as possible, place your new evangelists in classes that will equip them to build relationships and share Christ. Each session should last 90
minutes, including instruction, demonstration and
discussion. Classes should include material on:

The definition of evangelism
The evangelistic message
Why believers should get involved
How to build relationships with unbelievers
Developing a personal testimony
How to use gospel outlines
Evangelism and the Holy Spirit
Effective follow-up
The friendship evangelist's devotional life

Such topics will give each friendship evangelist an

adequate foundation for effective outreach. Obviously this book could serve as a primary resource for the class. Other helpful volumes include: *Lifestyle Evangelism* by Joseph Aldrich, Multnomah Press; *Friendship Evangelism* by Arthur McPhee, Zondervan; *Making Friends for Christ* by Wayne McDill, Broadman Press; *Someone Out There Needs Me* by Robert Tuttle, Jr., Zondervan; *Say It with Love* by Howard Hendricks, Victor Books; *The Master's Plan for Making Disciples* by Win and Charles Arn, Church Growth Press.

Organize ongoing prayer support for the evangelism program. Prayer is a must! It links friendship evangelism with the power of the Holy Spirit, our precious ally in outreach ministries. Every evangelist needs to be supported by faithful prayer warriors. They should be instructed to continually pray for God's anointing, direction and blessing. Pray that the Lord will open doors, lead evangelists to receptive people and fill their words with power. Churches involved in evangelism must be serious about prayer!

Begin by mobilizing existing prayer groups. Give leaders the names of evangelists as well as those of specific non-Christians. Make this a priority, for Satan will do anything and everything to keep people from Christ. Prayer will be a mighty weapon against his attacks.

As I mentioned previously, every friendship evangelist should enlist one or two specific prayer partners. Ask them to pray for the evangelist and his or her non-Christian friend. There are two benefits from such a program. First, it obviously provides friendship evangelists with necessary prayer support. But second, it gets more people involved in the evangelism ministry. This helps keep evangelism a high priority in any church.

Develop a network of program support. Friendship evangelists need program support. Churches must plan regular special events that will appeal to non-Christians. Concerts, videos, picnics and fellowship dinners provide good opportunities for believers to invite unbelieving friends. All events should be non-threatening, aimed at strengthening relationships while gently introducing new friends to other Christians. Throughout the year, schedule activities that are designed as support for friendship evangelism.

Also keep generating enthusiasm for the church outreach program. It is essential for maintaining ongoing commitment and involvement. One way to do this is by regularly scheduling 5-6 minutes in the worship service for an outreach update. Ask a friendship evangelist to share his or her experiences, stirring excitement for evangelism. Likewise, lift up ongoing concerns and prayer requests. This will keep the "good news" of friendship evangelism constantly before the people.

It is also important to regularly encourage friendship evangelists. One way to accomplish this is by occasionally checking with them to see how things are going. This should be the responsibility of the evangelism committee. Support, encouragement and caring can reignite the friendship evangelist when tough times come.

Always finish with follow-up. Never forget the central focus of the Great Commission. Jesus has commanded the church to "make disciples." After leading a person to belief in Christ, point the way to obedience. New believers need teaching in the foundational principles of Christian faith and practice. Without that, converts will, at best, experience shallow spirituality and nominal faith. The only way to fight this is through effective after-care. True evangelism is not complete until basic discipleship training occurs. When friendship evangelists commit themselves to outreach, follow-up is the last step.

The evangelism committee should decide on the format for follow-up. Will there be a new believers' class, a one-to-one program or a small group emphasis? Whatever the method, spell it out far in advance. The follow-up guide provided in chapter 8 will work well in any of these settings. Be *sure* follow-up occurs. It is a matter of life and death!

One more thing. Help new believers get established in the church. Make sure they meet new friends and get involved in church activities. Friendship is great glue. It will keep new people within the body for years to come. Do not assume that assimilation will happen naturally. Work hard at receiving and retaining new believers within the church family.

Friendship evangelism works. I know, because it was key to my own conversion. Any individual or church willing to get involved should get ready for a revolution. God will use it to transform countless lives, including yours. Are you ready to begin?

NOTES

1. George G. Hunter III, *The Contagious Congregation* (Nashville: Abingdon Press, 1979), p. 21.

2. George Sweezy, *Effective Evangelism* (New York: Harper and Row, 1953), p. 19.

3. Micheal Green, *Evangelism in the Early Church* (Grand Rapids, MI: WM. B. Eerdmans, 1970), p. 7.

4. G. Michael Cocoris, *Evangelism: A Biblical Approach* (Chicago: Moody Press, 1984), p. 14.

5. John C. Chapman, *Know and Tell the Gospel* (Colorado Springs: NavPress, 1985), p. 13.

6. Edward R. Dayton and David A. Fraser, *Planning Strategies for World Evangelization* (Grand Rapids, MI: WM. B. Eerdmans, 1980), p. 80.

7. This material is taken from Dr. C. Peter Wagner's lectures on church growth at Fuller Theological Seminary.

8. Rebecca Pippert, *Out of the Salt Shaker and Into the World*, (Downers Grove, IL: Intervarsity Press, 1979), pp. 88ff.

9. John Adams and Scott Rigby, "Impact 88: A Study of Evangelism in the Metropolitan Area" (An unpublished study).

10. A helpful study on spiritual gifts is important for Christians. C. Peter Wagner's book, *Your Spiritual Gifts Can Help Your Church Grow*, by Tyndale, is a good resource.

11. The Charles E. Fuller Institute of Evangelism and Church Growth offers an excellent resource for discovering your spiritual gifts. It is an audio tape and workbook set by C. Peter Wagner called *Spiritual Gifts and Church Growth*.

12. C. Peter Wagner, *Your Spiritual Gifts Can Help Your Church Grow* (Wheaton, IL: Tyndale House Publishers, 1979), p. 77.

13. J.R.W. Stott, *Christian Mission in the Modern World* (Downers Grove, IL: Intervarsity Press, 1975), p. 54–55.

14. David Watson, *How to Find God* (Wheaton, IL: Harold Shaw Publishers, 1977), p. 144.

15. Watson, p. 145.

16. Watson, p. 196.

17. James Kennedy, *Evangelism Explosion* (Wheaton, IL: Tyndale House Publishers, 1983), p. 4.

18. Jim Wallis, *An Agenda for Biblical People* (New York: Harper and Row Publishers, Inc., 1984), p. 9.

19. Dietrich Bonhoeffer, *The Cost of Discipleship* (New York: The MacMillan Company, 1976), p. 74.

20. J.I. Packer, *Evangelism and the Sovereignty of God* (Downers Grove, IL: Intervarsity Press, 1961), p. 26.

21. Micheal Green, *Evangelism in the Early Church* (Grand Rapids, MI: WM. B. Eerdmans, 1970), p. 7.

22. C. Peter Wagner, *Stop the World, I Want to Get Off* (Pasadena, CA: William Carey Library Publishers, 1979), p. 21.

23. Leighton Ford, *The Christian Persuader* (New York: Harper and Row Publishers, Inc., 1966), p. 29.

24. Micheal Green, *I Believe in the Holy Spirit* (Grand Rapids, MI: WM. B. Eerdmans, 1975), p. 65.

25. Raymond C. Ortlund, *Let the Church Be the Church* (Waco, TX: Word, Inc., 1983), p. 9–11.

26. David Watson, *I Believe in the Church* (Grand Rapids, MI: WM. B. Eerdmans, 1978), p. 66.

27. Robert Webber, *Worship Old and New* (Grand Rapids, MI: Zondervan Publishing House, 1972), p. 42.

28. E.M. Bounds, *Power Through Prayer* (Grand Rapids, MI: Baker Book House, 1972), p. 42.

29. David Watson, *I Believe in Evangelism* (Grand Rapids, MI: WM. B. Eerdmans, 1976), p. 61.

30. Richard K. Curtis, *They Call Him Mr. Moody* (Grand Rapids, MI: WM. B. Eerdmans, 1962), p. 156.

31. Found in the tape/workbook resource *Spiritual gifts and Church Growth.*

32. A.B. Simpson, *The Holy Spirit* (Camp Hill, PA: Christian Publications, n.d.), p. 83–84.

33. A.W. Thompson, *A.B. Simpson: His Life and Work* (Camp Hill, PA: Christian Publications, 1960), p. 63–71.

34. Edmund Fuller and B. Jo Kinnick, *Adventures in American Literature*, Vol. 2 (San Diego, CA: Harcourt Brace Jovanovich, Inc., 1963), pp. 319–324.

35. Win Arn, ed., *The Pastor's Church Growth Handbook*, Vol. 2 (Corunna, IN: Church Growth Center, 1982), pp. 3–36.

36. David Watson, *I Believe in Evangelism*, p. 83.

37. Paul Orjala, *Get Ready to Grow.* (Kansas City, MO: Beacon Hill Press of Kansas City, 1978), p. 58.

38. Win Arn, *The Pastor's Church Growth Handbook*, Vol. 1 (Corunna, IN: Church Growth Center, 1979) pp. 95–109.

39. Ted Engstrom with Robert Classon, *The Fine Art of Friendship* (Nashville, TN: Thomas Nelson, Inc., Publishers, 1985), p. 20–21.

40. This is an abbreviated version of similar tract of the same name available from the Billy Graham Association.

41. David Watson, *How to Find God* (Wheaton, IL: Harold Shaw Publishers, 1976), p. 144.

42. Taken from the leaflet "Four Things You Want to Know," published by the International Bible Society.